In the realm of darkness mercy is a weapon of the weak.
Salvation is damned by the dark side and denied by

The Deadman.

The iron gates of the underworld have been welded shut

by the taker of souls,

The Apocalyptic Warrior.

There is no escape now,

for in the end there is only the immortal darkness.

There is no one else who has garnered the unanimous respect that The Deadman has attained. When asked "Who has the most respect in the business?" incredibly, only one name pops up on everyone's list—Undertaker.

I was so honored to have fought both with Undertaker in the Ministry of Darkness and against him for the WWE Title as JBL. I have fought this icon, literally, hundreds of times. My record is about as good as the Washington Generals against the Globetrotters which helps me realize that every time the bell rang, Undertaker was there to perform at a level at which most only dream of performing.

My first live televised match was against Undertaker. It was the same match where Mankind debuted on *Monday Night Raw*—the night after Undertaker had a brutal *WrestleMania* match with Diesel. When I started, and for many years after, the test for a new talent was a match with Undertaker. If a talent could keep up, or at least mostly keep up, with Undertaker for a premier match on *Raw* then that talent deserved to be in WWE.

This rite of passage was carried out month after month and year after year with Undertaker being the testing ground both for new talent and, at the same time, the main event storylines. When Undertaker was not in the main event he was always the "break the glass" scenario if something wasn't working.

In my opinion, the backbone of WWE for over two decades has been Undertaker. Others have come and gone, and some have come back again, but there has been one constant—the Phenom from Death Valley.

No streak will ever match Undertaker's *WrestleMania* streak, but more important to all of us who have been in WWE for so long and consider it family, is the streak Undertaker has had as the heart and soul of this business.

There will never be another like him; I am just happy I got to be a part of the era that he helped create.

I've been blessed for the last twenty-plus years to have been in the ring with the best this business has ever seen. From the Hulk Hogan era to the Attitude Era to the current era, I can say without a moment's hesitation that Undertaker is the best to have ever performed in this business.

John Bradshaw Layfield

INTRODUCTION

A legend unlike any other, Undertaker has spent a quarter century vanquishing the poor souls of sports-entertainment's most storied names. Along the way, he has gained an unmatched measure of admiration from fans and an undeniable level of respect from those who have dared to enter his yard.

The pages that follow take you on a journey that spans over twenty-five years and illustrates how the most ominous figure in WWE history became one of sports-entertainment's greatest legends.

From Undertaker's turbulent relationship with Paul Bearer to his fiery bond with his brother, Kane, you will gain a complete understanding of the life events that helped shape The Deadman WWE fans see today. Additionally, you'll experience blow-by-blow accounts of Undertaker's greatest matches and dissect his most heated rivalries. And of course, no tome of Undertaker's career would be complete without an in-depth look at The Phenom's monumental *WrestleMania* successes. From Jimmy "Superfly" Snuka to Triple H to Bray Wyatt, see how Undertaker has created a legacy that will live for generations to come.

This is his story. The story of how on a cold night in November 1990, a mysterious figure emerged and immediately made an entire industry stand up and take notice. The decades-long story of a preternatural force dominating everything put in his path. The story of a demon from Death Valley becoming one of the most recognizable names in sports-entertainment history. The story of Undertaker.

DEBUT OF THE DEADMAN

NOVEMBER 22, 1990

When the Ultimate Warrior eliminated Mr. Perfect to become the sole survivor in the opening match of *Survivor Series*, the capacity crowd in Connecticut's capitol city worked themselves into a seemingly unstoppable frenzy. But within minutes of Warrior's thrilling victory, a sudden and unexpected hush fell over the arena when Ted DiBiase unveiled the final member of his Million Dollar Team.

Hailing from Death Valley, the dark and mysterious figure slowly emerged. Fans looked on in awe as the expressionless newcomer, clad in black and grey, sauntered to the ring alongside manager Brother Love. The dark circles under his eyes reinforced his incredibly imposing appearance. Even before he stepped foot in the ring, it was clear he was different from the mortals with which he was about to share the stage. He was unlike anything anybody had ever seen before in WWE. He was Undertaker.

The wake-like silence that overcame the Hartford Civic Center intensified when Undertaker's eerie funeral procession entrance music finally came to an end. Mouths agape, fans continued to look on in disbelief as members of The Dream Team began to fear the worst.

Bret "Hit Man" Hart was the first unlucky soul on Dusty Rhodes's Dream Team to try to take down The Deadman, but when his offense proved futile, he quickly tagged in Jim "The Anvil" Neidhart. Like Hart, Neidhart was incapable of inflicting any pain to Undertaker and within seconds, tagged in Koko B. Ware.

Judging from his energy level, "The Birdman" believed he possessed the skill to accomplish what his partners couldn't. Unfortunately for Koko, however, his high energy failed to equate to anything worthwhile. Within thirty seconds of being in the ring, "The Birdman" found himself on the receiving end of the first-ever Tombstone piledriver.

As Undertaker rolled Koko's nearly lifeless body from the ring, the remaining members of The Dream Team huddled in their corner, wondering if there was any stopping this awesome newcomer. As they soon learned, the only thing standing between them and complete annihilation was The Deadman's undying loyalty to his manager.

After eliminating Rhodes from the match, thanks in large part to a devastating double axe handle from the top rope, Undertaker dismissed "The American Dream" over the top rope and onto the arena floor. Once there, Brother Love began to assault the downed Rhodes with kicks of his own. The weak blows managed to anger "The American Dream" more than anything else, and it wasn't long before Rhodes was threatening to return the favor. Seeing his manager in peril, Undertaker quickly exited the ring and rushed to Brother Love's aid. The Deadman's allegiance saved his manager from certain doom, but in the process also resulted in Undertaker being eliminated from the match via countout.

In the end, DiBiase was able to pin Hart to become the match's sole survivor. In reality, though, the record books only shed a sliver of light on what really happened on that Thanksgiving night in 1990. On this evening, the big story coming out of *Survivor Series* was the introduction of Undertaker, an otherworldly force that would go on to make life a living hell for WWE Superstars for more than two decades.

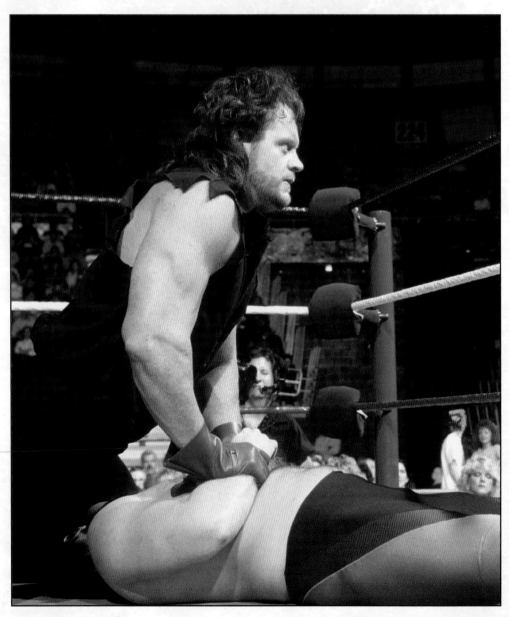

ALSO ON NOVEMBER 22, 1990

- WWE Champion, Ultimate Warrior
- WWE Intercontinental Champion, Mr. Perfect
- WWE World Tag Team Champions, Hart Foundation

ALSO IN 1990

- Hulk Hogan won the *Royal Rumble*.
- *WrestleMania* was held outside the United States for the first time when Toronto's SkyDome hosted the annual extravaganza.
- Vader debuted in WCW.
- Robocop saved Sting from an attack at the hands of the Four Horsemen.
- The last-ever AWA Champion, Larry Zbyszko, was stripped of the title, marking the ceremonial end of the promotion.
- Bo Dallas was born.

PAUL BEARER

"You ain't seen nothing yet," Brother Love told fans following Undertaker's impressive debut at *Survivor Series*. The prophetic statement proved to be the truest words the loud-mouthed manager ever uttered, as The Deadman spent the next several weeks burying all challengers. After each victory, Undertaker paid final respects to his opponents by showering their fallen bodies with crumpled rose petals.

Despite Undertaker's impactful first few months, Brother Love claimed he wasn't able to give the grim newcomer the love he needed to truly succeed in WWE. So instead of giving a cursory effort as Undertaker's manager, Brother Love handed over the reins to Paul Bearer, a man whose chilling background made him far better equipped to guide the career of such an ominous force.

A mortician by trade, Paul Bearer proved to be the perfect complement to Undertaker's incredibly macabre presence. His pale skin, plodding walk, and high-pitched voice instilled fear in arenas well before Undertaker even emerged from the back. And with Bearer serving as The Deadman's caretaker, Undertaker solidified himself as a legitimate long-term threat in WWE. Before long, The Phenom's level of competition elevated from the likes of Mario Mancini and William Ford to future Hall of Famers Jimmy "Superfly" Snuka and "Hacksaw" Jim Duggan. But regardless of each opponent's skill level, the result always remained the same: victory for the Undertaker.

BEARER THE BETRAYER

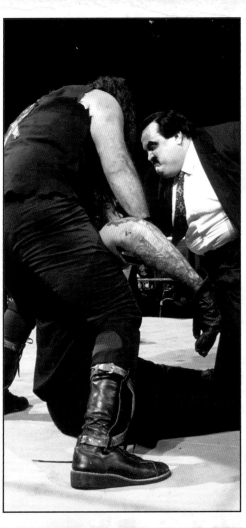

For more than five years, the Paul Bearer-led Undertaker loomed over WWE as one of the most physically and mentally imposing competitors of all time. Not even the great Hulk Hogan could solve The Deadman, who beat The Hulkster for the WWE Championship at *Survivor Series* 1991. But despite their success, the seemingly unbreakable bond between Bearer and Undertaker was inexplicably shattered in the summer of 1996. While standing in The Deadman's corner for his *SummerSlam* Boiler Room Brawl with Mankind, Bearer shocked the sports-entertainment world when he whacked Undertaker with his signature urn.

Paul Bearer's Judas-like act not only marked the end of the manager's union with Undertaker, but also served as the launching pad for his alliance with the deranged Mankind. Over the next several months, Bearer and Mankind embarked on a ruthless assault designed to ultimately rid WWE of The Phenom. The callous duo even enlisted the help of Vader and The Executioner. Despite their best efforts, however, Bearer's army was unable to bury The Deadman.

When his attempts to end Undertaker proved fruitless, Bearer turned to Plan B: blackmail. Claiming he had knowledge of a dark secret from The Deadman's past, Bearer forced Undertaker to fall back under his leadership, otherwise the manager threatened to reveal the skeletons that resided in The Phenom's closet. The plan worked. A helpless Undertaker eventually succumbed to Bearer's demands, albeit briefly.

When an exasperated Undertaker finally broke away from Bearer, the manager made good on his promise to reveal The Deadman's secret. According to Bearer, a young Undertaker set fire to his family's funeral parlor, a fire that was believed to have killed The Deadman's mother, father, and brother, Kane. In reality, though, Bearer revealed that Kane was, in fact, alive and coming for Undertaker.

Just as he did for Undertaker years earlier, Paul Bearer led the nascent days of Kane's career with great brilliance. Realizing he was pulling the strings for one of the most dominant forces to ever lace a pair of boots, Bearer turned Kane loose on many of WWE's top stars, including Ahmed Johnson and Vader. As expected, Kane made short work of whoever Bearer put in front of him, en route to a showdown with Undertaker at *WrestleMania XIV*.

UNDERTAKER REUNION

Amazingly, Paul Bearer and Undertaker reunited in late 1998 when the manager surprisingly helped The Deadman in his *Judgment Day* match against Kane. The reconciled pairing proved to be more evil than ever before. As founding members of the demonic Ministry of Darkness, Bearer and Undertaker engaged in unthinkable actions that sent fear through arenas and locker rooms alike. The most diabolical plans Bearer and Undertaker unleashed saw the duo attempt to bury and embalm Stone Cold Steve Austin alive.

In the years that followed, Paul Bearer made sporadic appearances at The Phenom's side, including at *WrestleMania XX* when The Deadman persona returned to WWE after years of Undertaker competing as the American Bad Ass. More than a decade after their original pairing on WWE television, and many ups and downs, the event proved that Paul Bearer would forever be synonymous with the success of Undertaker.

A SADISTIC RECONCILIATION

It was with Kane that Paul Bearer enjoyed his final role as an active member of the WWE roster. In addition to being by the Big Red Monster's side for portions of his 2010 World Heavyweight Championship reign, Bearer briefly aided the Big Red monster during his 2012 rivalry with Randy Orton. And fittingly, it was Kane who ultimately dismissed Paul Bearer from WWE when he rolled the wheelchair-ridden manager into an oversized freezer.

Like Undertaker, Kane's relationship with Paul Bearer was made up of many turbulent peaks and valleys. But despite their oft-rocky relationship, it's undeniable that much of Kane's success can be directly traced to his relationship with Paul Bearer.

DEATH

Sadly, the wrestling world lost Paul Bearer when the longtime manager passed away in March 2013. But even in death, Bearer managed to be a driving force behind Undertaker's incredible success.

In the weeks following Bearer's passing, CM Punk went to great lengths to dishonor the memory of Undertaker's longtime friend and manager. The Straightedge Superstar even went so far as to empty the contents of Bearer's urn over a prone Undertaker's body. In the end, however, the disgusting deeds failed to derail Undertaker. Instead, The Phenom used Punk's actions as motivation to destroy the disrespectful Superstar at *WrestleMania 29*.

The following year, Paul Bearer took his rightful place in the WWE Hall of Fame. The emotional ceremony saw Kane introduce Bearer's sons, Michael and Daniel Moody, to accept the honor on their father's behalf. Fittingly, the induction ended with Undertaker paying his final tribute to Bearer, kneeling and holding the famous urn high in the air.

OVERVIEW

Height: 5'10

First appearance: February 1991

Superstars managed: Undertaker, Kane, Mankind, Vader, The Executioner

2014 Hall of Fame inductee

FUNERAL PARLOR

Hosted by Paul Bearer, *The Funeral Parlor* interview segment served as the site of some of WWE's most memorable moments, including Undertaker locking the Ultimate Warrior inside an airtight casket and longtime WCW star Ric Flair confronting Hulk Hogan.

THE URN

The power of the urn is both mysterious and undeniable. For more than two decades, Superstars have tried to destroy its paranormal powers. But with each futile attempt, the mystical connection between the urn and Undertaker has grown even greater.

JANUARY 22, 1994, ROYAL RUMBLE

A mysterious green smoke emerged from the urn after Yokozuna's henchmen attacked Undertaker at the *Royal Rumble*. Many believed the smoke symbolized The Deadman's power exiting his body as he was rolled into the ringside casket.

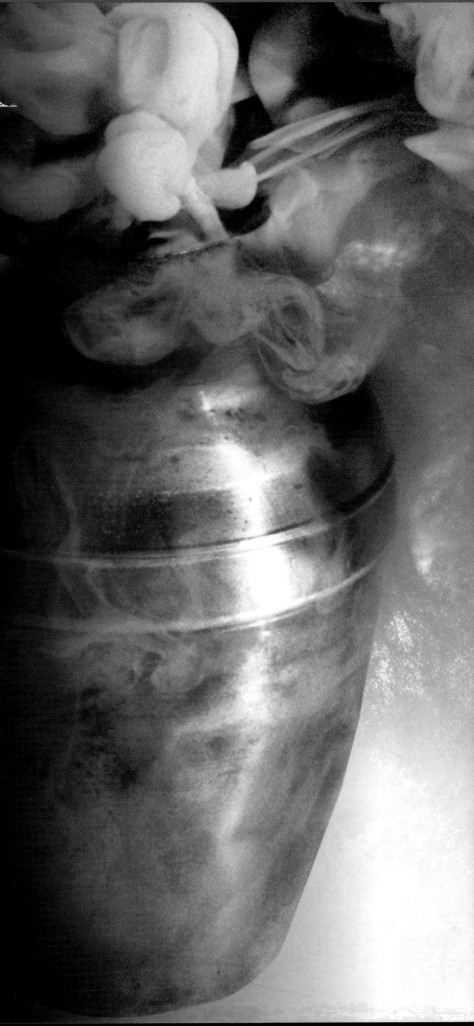

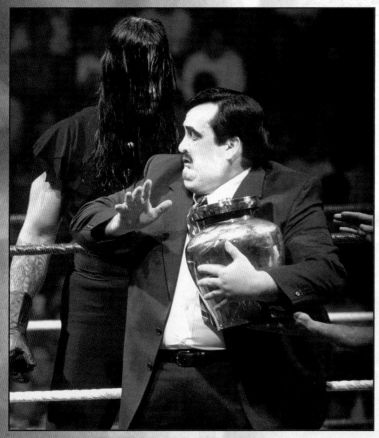

AUGUST 29, 1994, *SUMMERSLAM*

With Undertaker unseen for much of 1994, Paul Bearer used the power of an oversized urn to summon The Deadman back into action at *SummerSlam*.

When Kama stole Undertaker's urn at *WrestleMania XI*, not only did he commandeer the source of much of The Phenom's powers, he also poured salt in the wound when he melted down The Deadman's guiding light and turned it into an oversized gold necklace.

Undertaker spent much of the summer trying to regain his coveted urn, but despite defeating Kama at each turn, the Supreme Fighting Machine somehow managed to get away with its remnants each time. Finally in December 1997, Undertaker appeared to regain the source of his power, but just as he gave it to Paul Bearer, King Mabel invaded and stole the urn for himself. The Deadman finally regained the urn's remnants at *In Your House: Seasons Beatings* when he defeated King Mabel in a Casket Match.

AUGUST 18, 1996, *SUMMERSLAM*

Paul Bearer broke his near lifelong bond with Undertaker at *SummerSlam* when he used the urn to knock The Deadman unconscious. The shocking betrayal marked the end of Bearer's union with Undertaker and the beginning of his devious alliance with Mankind.

THE GRAVEST CHALLENGE

After months of carnage created at the hand of The Deadman, the question on everybody's minds wasn't *if* Undertaker would one day become WWE Champion. Rather, fans began to wonder *when* Undertaker would become WWE Champion.

The Phenom took a giant step toward answering that question on a November 1991 edition of *The Funeral Parlor*. While WWE Champion Hulk Hogan was engaged in a war of words with Ric Flair, The Deadman stealthily slipped from a nearby casket and clobbered The Hulkster with Paul Bearer's signature urn. From there, both Undertaker and Flair further assaulted the fallen champion, who had little chance against the brutal two-on-one attack.

Luckily for Hogan, the sinister assault was eventually thwarted when Randy Savage and Roddy Piper rushed to The Hulkster's aid. Savage and Piper were able to stop the attack, but were unsuccessful in ridding the scene of Undertaker. Rather than run, The Deadman simply stood over Hogan's carcass, showing that he wasn't afraid of anybody or anything. Before finally departing, Undertaker showed the champ the ultimate sign of disrespect by ripping the crucifix from his neck and carelessly dropping it on his chest.

As a result of *The Funeral Parlor* incident, Hogan agreed to put his WWE Championship on the line against Undertaker at *Survivor Series*. Officially dubbed "The Gravest Challenge," the match was seen by many as an unwinnable situation for The Hulkster. Never before had anybody defeated The Phenom and, given the abuse Hogan endured

less than two weeks prior at his hands, the champ certainly was not in a favorable position. But that didn't stop Hogan from seeking revenge from The Deadman.

The capacity crowd was firmly in The Hulkster's corner, but despite their undying support, the champ could barely muster any offense on Undertaker. Finally, after ten minutes of dominating the action, the challenger looked to put Hogan out of his misery by delivering a thunderous Tombstone. Silence fell over the capacity crowd, who assumed they were watching the end of Hulkamania. But miraculously, Hogan jumped right up from the Tombstone and managed to go on the offensive.

This was the Hulkster the fans hoped to see on this night. And in typical Hogan fashion, the champ landed a Big Boot to Undertaker's chin before attempting to go for his patented leg drop. But before Hogan could execute the maneuver, he became distracted by Paul Bearer at ringside. The interference gave Undertaker the opportunity to get to his feet and scoop up an unsuspecting Hogan for yet another Tombstone. This time, the impact of the Deadman's Tombstone was compounded by a foreign object placed on the mat by a meddling Ric Flair.

"Hulkamania is dead, it is dead! Long live the Undertaker," shouted commentator Bobby "The Brain" Heenan as the referee counted to three and awarded the match and WWE Championship to Undertaker. Many fans looked on in disbelief, while others cried at the sight of Undertaker leaving the arena with the title in tow as their hero was left a crumpled mess in the middle of the ring.

"Hulkamania is dead, it is dead!
Long live the Undertaker,"
—Commentator Bobby "The Brain" Heenen

THIS TUESDAY IN TEXAS

Within minutes of losing the WWE Championship, Hulk Hogan was given an audience with WWE President Jack Tunney, proving that despite no longer having the gold, The Hulkster still had plenty of stroke. And before the next *Survivor Series* match got underway, Tunney had told the viewing audience that a rematch would take place at the earliest possible date. That date turned out to be the following Tuesday in Texas.

Being forced to defend his newly-won WWE Championship less than a week after capturing the prize didn't faze Undertaker. Rather, the new champ welcomed the opportunity. According to The Deadman, Hulkamania died at *Survivor Series* and *This Tuesday in Texas* was going to be the burial. The opening moments of the rematch, however, told a different story.

Unlike their original confrontation, much of the rematch's early moments belonged to Hogan. The Hulkster was even able to fend off a two-on-one attack when Paul Bearer entered the fray. It wasn't until the action spilled out to the arena floor several minutes into the match that Undertaker was able to gain any sort of sustained upper hand.

Once back in the ring, the action continued at a back-and-forth pace until finally, Hogan began to "hulk up," which traditionally meant the beginning of the end for his opponent. This time, though, The Hulkster's concentration shifted when Ric Flair came to ringside. Tunney tried to stop "The Nature Boy," but his authority failed to intimidate Flair. Hoping to avoid a repeat of what happened at *Survivor Series*, Hogan whacked Flair, sending "The Nature Boy" atop Tunney and subsequently crashing to the arena floor.

Hogan climbed back into the ring, where the action resumed while Tunney lay unconscious on the outside. With the WWE President out cold,

Paul Bearer saw his opening. The manager climbed to the ring apron and swung his urn at Hogan, who was being held by Undertaker. At the last moment, however, The Hulkster sidestepped the dastardly deed, resulting in The Deadman absorbing the crushing blow.

With Undertaker reeling, Hogan snatched the urn from Bearer's clutches and emptied its contents onto the mat. He then grabbed a handful of ashes and threw them directly into Undertaker's eyes, temporarily blinding him. The Deadman's state of confusion was all Hogan needed to scoop Undertaker from behind for the pin and win.

The victory marked the beginning of Hogan's fourth WWE Championship reign, which was also his shortest. Just days after the match, President Tunney took to WWE TV to make what he knew would be a very difficult announcement.

"As President of WWE, I am fully aware that the decisions of this office are not always popular, and that this one will be no exception," began a stern-faced Tunney. "However, I cannot stand idly by and take little action in the face of such grievous circumstances. This past Tuesday in Texas, during the Undertaker-Hulk Hogan Championship Match, I witnessed with my own eyes what I believe was a flagrant and far-reaching oversight on the part of the referee. Now, the referee's decision is final; I will not challenge his official decision. However, under these circumstances, I have little choice but to decree the [WWE] Title vacant."

And with that ruling by President Jack Tunney, the ongoing saga between Undertaker and Hulk Hogan, and their quest for the WWE Championship, reached its controversial conclusion; that is until the two Superstars squared off again for WWE's ultimate prize more than a decade later.

SIGNATURE MOVES

Ever since Undertaker brutally drove Koko B. Ware into the mat at *Survivor Series 1990*, the Tombstone has been recognized as one of the most feared signature moves in sports-entertainment history. And since that fateful night, The Deadman has added even more maneuvers to his nearly endless offensive repertoire, which over the years has become synonymous with Undertaker's success.

March 24, 1991, *WrestleMania VII:* Undertaker kicks off his amazing *WrestleMania* undefeated streak with a Tombstone on Jimmy Snuka.

May 29, 1995, *Raw:* Undertaker flattens Jeff Jarrett with a Tombstone to win a King of the Ring qualifying match.

March 17, 2002, *WrestleMania X8*: Ric Flair finds himself on the wrong end of a Tombstone at *WrestleMania X8*.

March 30, 2008, *WrestleMania XXIV:* The Rated-R Superstar is stopped in his tracks by The Deadman's Tombstone at *WrestleMania XXIV*.

OLD SCHOOL

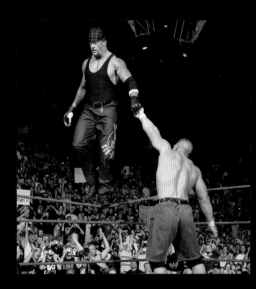

October 21, 2001, *No Mercy***:** Booker T is in awe of The Phenom's cat-like agility.

January 22, 2008, *SmackDown***:** Not even the nearly five hundred pound frame of Big Daddy V was immune to Old School.

July 27, 2003, *Vengeance***:** Undertaker delivers Old School to John Cena in a rare pay-per-view encounter between the two legends.

April 1, 2012, *WrestleMania XXVIII***:** Undertaker delivers Old School to Triple H inside Hell in a Cell.

CHOKESLAM

August 17, 2008, *SummerSlam*: A Deadman Chokeslam sends Edge out of the ring and through a table.

January 18, 1998, *Royal Rumble*: For Shawn Michaels, there's no escaping the clutches of Undertaker's massive grip.

May 21, 2000, *Judgment Day*: Mr. McMahon watches as a Chokeslam flattens his son, Shane.

April 21, 2008, *Raw*: Undertaker delivers a dual Chokeslam to Randy Orton and JBL.

LAST RIDE

June 11, 2001, *Raw*: All the gold medals in the world can't save Kurt Angle from the Last Ride.

September 19, 2002, *SmackDown*: Matt Hardy learns the hard way never to interrupt Undertaker.

HELL'S GATE

April 11, 2008, *SmackDown*: Festus can't fight his way free from The Phenom's Hell's Gate.

January 25, 2008, *SmackDown*: Big Daddy V was the first-ever poor soul to be on the receiving end of Undertaker's Hell's Gate.

BIG BOOT

August 18, 1997, *Raw*: Undertaker drops Triple H with a Big Boot to the face.

March 23, 1997, *WrestleMania 13*: Dueling Big Boots by Undertaker and Sycho Sid.

December 9, 2001, *Vengeance*: RVD exits the ring the hard way, thanks to a Big Boot by The Deadman.

GUILLOTINE LEG DROP

October 9, 2007, *SmackDown*: MVP feels the wrath of an Undertaker Guillotine Leg Drop.

April 29, 2007, *Backlash*: Undertaker nails Batista with the Guillotine Leg Drop.

LEAPING CLOTHESLINE

February 12, 2001,
Raw: Undertaker
takes to the skies to
bring down Edge.

August 27, 1995, *SummerSlam:* The Deadman's leaping clothesline is too much for Kama to withstand.

April 15, 2002, *Raw:* Undertaker's leaping clothesline drops Stone Cold Steve Austin.

PLANCHA

February 23, 2003, *No Way Out*: Jaws drop as Undertaker leaps over the top rope onto A-Train and Paul Heyman.

March 30, 2008, *WrestleMania XXIV*: Edge absorbs the blow of a flying Phenom.

April 5, 2009, *WrestleMania XXV*: Undertaker puts his own body on the line in his match against Shawn Michaels.

GOOD AND EVIL

For some Superstars, an appearance on Paul Bearer's *Funeral Parlor* meant the opportunity to speak their minds on a powerful platform that reached millions of fans worldwide. For the Ultimate Warrior, however, his Spring, 1991 appearance was not only disturbing, it also set a diabolical plan into motion designed to crush the soul of the popular face-painted Superstar.

The sinister scheme began when Undertaker emerged from a nearby casket and attacked an unsuspecting Warrior from behind. After striking his target with the urn, The Deadman proceeded to lock the Warrior inside an airtight casket. WWE officials rushed from the back to try to pry the casket open. But as they struggled, and the seconds turned to minutes, everybody began to fear the worst—this was the end of the Warrior.

After several anxious moments, officials were finally able to crack the casket. A motionless Warrior rested inside. The casket's interior showed signs of a fight; clearly Warrior tried to claw his way free before taking what appeared to be his final breath. As fans began to grasp the severity of what they just witnessed, the seemingly unthinkable happened inside the casket. Ultimate Warrior miraculously began to show signs of life.

Amazingly, Warrior was able to recover from Undertaker's heinous actions. But little did he realize that he was already deeply immersed in the next phase of The Deadman's sadistic plan.

Following the attack, longtime fan favorite Jake "The Snake" Roberts appeared on *The Funeral Parlor* to offer his services to the Ultimate Warrior. Roberts told Warrior he could help him overcome any fears he may have of Undertaker. Warrior agreed to work with the Snake, who put the popular Superstar through a series of unconventional tests designed to arm him with knowledge of the dark side. Upon completing the tasks, Roberts assured Warrior he'd be prepared for anything Undertaker could possibly dish out.

The first two tests saw Warrior once again locked inside a casket, followed by being buried up to his neck in a grave. And despite the grim nature of each task, Warrior passed with relative ease. The third and final test, however, was designed to be impossible. Roberts locked Warrior in a dark chamber filled with

snakes and told him that the answers he needed were in a chest found in the center of the room. After carefully navigating his way through the serpent-filled space, Warrior reached the chest and opened it wide. The promised answers, however, were not inside. Instead, he was met by a venomous cobra, which bit Warrior on the face.

Never trust a snake

Poison coursed through Warrior's veins as he fell to the floor. With the last remaining traces of energy he had left, the fading Superstar attempted to crawl for safety. But as he dragged his nearly lifeless body across the floor, the only thing Warrior could find was the boot of the Undertaker. Realizing certain doom was near, Warrior turned and slowly extended his hand to Roberts for help. But the Snake offered no assistance.

"Never trust a snake," Roberts told the wounded Warrior, revealing his shocking allegiance to Undertaker in the process. The elaborate plan's success solidified Undertaker as one of the most ruthless competitors WWE had ever seen. Not only was he able to convert Roberts to the dark side, but The Deadman also left the Ultimate Warrior a shell of his former self. The disoriented Warrior never fully rebounded from Undertaker's plot and ultimately took an extended sabbatical from WWE shortly thereafter.

A SAVAGE ATTACK

Following the systematic dismantling of Warrior's psyche, Undertaker and Roberts continued to terrorize the minds of WWE's locker room. And while presumably every Superstar trembled at the thought of being targeted by The Deadman and Roberts, the devious duo eventually revealed that they only had eyes for one very popular couple: Randy "Macho Man" Savage and Miss Elizabeth.

The entire sports-entertainment community rejoiced when Savage and Elizabeth offered an open invitation to their wedding at *SummerSlam 1991*. But while the world eagerly awaited the pending nuptials, Undertaker and Roberts began to plot their next devious plan, which was ultimately unveiled at the newlyweds' wedding reception.

Miss Elizabeth had never looked more beautiful, and Savage never more happy. Surrounded by family and friends, the new husband and wife celebrated their union with a night that could not have been more perfect. But unfortunately for them, their tender evening turned to terror when they began to open the gifts. An unsuspecting Elizabeth screeched in fright when she unwrapped a box containing a king cobra. Looking to strike, the snake darted toward Savage and Elizabeth, who both scurried for safety. But before the newlyweds could get too far, Undertaker rushed the scene and flattened Savage with the urn.

As Macho Man tried to recover, Roberts taunted Elizabeth with the snake. The horrified bride tried to get away, but Roberts and his serpent continued to inch closer. Luckily for Elizabeth, Sid soon emerged and drove away Undertaker, Roberts, and the cobra. But the damage had been done. The wedding reception was ruined, and The Deadman and the Snake further cemented their position as the most heartless duo in all of WWE.

AN HONORABLE UNDERTAKER

Coming off the heels of the Savage/Elizabeth wedding reception, the idea of Undertaker being capable of doing the right thing seemed completely unfathomable. But as Roberts's obsession with destroying Savage and Elizabeth intensified, The Deadman's conscience finally kicked in.

After losing to Savage on *Saturday Night's Main Event*, Roberts sought vengeance by going after Macho Man and Elizabeth with a foreign object found at ringside. But before the Snake could connect, Undertaker stepped in and derailed the attack. Roberts looked at The Deadman in shock; his actions contradicted everything the duo had stood for up to that point.

Looking for answers, a furious Roberts asked Undertaker whose side he was on. Expressionless, The Deadman spoke just two words that would forever change how WWE and its fans would look at him, "Not yours!"

With that simple statement, Undertaker would go on to become one of the most adored Superstars in WWE history. No longer was he fueled by evil intentions and the misery of others. Rather, by shedding himself of the slithering Snake, The Deadman found power in ridding WWE of its most evil figures, starting with Roberts at *WrestleMania VIII*.

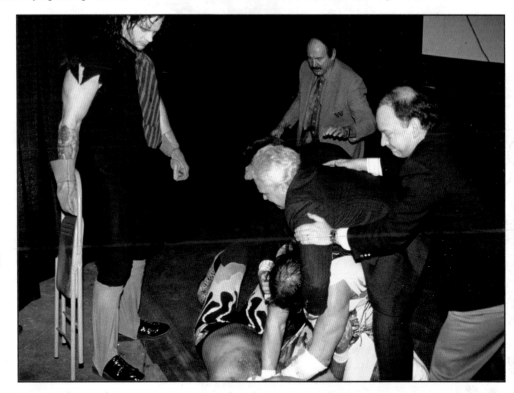

THE CONQUERING OF GIANTS

After discarding Roberts at *WrestleMania*, Undertaker spent the next year almost exclusively fending off Harvey Wippleman charges, each one more massive than the other. The first to try his hand at The Deadman was Kamala. But despite his best efforts, the Ugandan Giant was unable to end Undertaker, forcing Wippleman to come up with a bigger and badder strategy, which he unveiled at the *Royal Rumble*.

After eliminating a host of Superstars from the *Royal Rumble* match, including Ted DiBiase and The Berzerker, Undertaker appeared to be among the favorites to win the event. But then, out of nowhere, came an eight-foot monster lumbering down the aisle with Wippleman in tow. The never-before-seen giant dwarfed Undertaker and tossed him around like a ragdoll, eliminating The Deadman from the match in the process. Never before had the Undertaker been manhandled in such a fashion.

Wippleman's newcomer was revealed to be Giant Gonzales, and his sole mission was to destroy Undertaker. Unfortunately for Wippleman and his oversized client, however, their mission was a complete disaster. Undertaker went on to defeat Giant Gonzales at *WrestleMania IX* and again at *SummerSlam*.

BE NOT PROUD

With a win over the biggest competitor to ever grace a WWE ring, it appeared as though no *single* man could ever beat Undertaker. And with that fact in mind, the devious Mr. Fuji ensured his man, WWE Champion Yokozuna, had plenty of backup for his Casket Match against The Deadman at the 1994 *Royal Rumble*.

Heading into the match, it was revealed that Yokozuna was terrified of caskets which, when coupled with Undertaker's proficiency in Casket Matches, made this one of the rare occasions when the WWE Champion was considered the underdog going in. And when the match started, Undertaker looked every bit the favorite, controlling much of the early moments. It wasn't until Yokozuna tossed a handful of salt into The Deadman's eyes that the champ was able to gain any sort of sustained offense. But despite Yokozuna's best efforts, The Deadman refused to stay down. And it wasn't long before Undertaker was back in control.

Following a Chokeslam and DDT to Yokozuna, Undertaker rolled the mighty champion into the casket, en route to certain victory. But before he could close the lid, Crush ran down and attacked The Deadman. Undertaker was able to fend off the assault, but before he could get back to the task at hand, even more Superstars ran down to attack The Deadman. Before long, Undertaker was also dealing with Bam Bam Bigelow, Diesel, The Great Kabuki, Genichiro Tenryu, Jeff Jarrett, Adam Bomb, and The Headshrinkers.

Amazingly, Undertaker was able to fend off the nine-on-one attack. That is, until Yokozuna reemerged from the casket and struck The Deadman over the head with the urn. The champ and his henchmen then rolled Undertaker into the casket, as a mysterious green smoke came pouring from the dented urn.

With the lid closed and the match now over, Yokozuna's gang of thugs began to bring the casket back as a trophy. But before they could get too far, Undertaker's signature gong thundered throughout the arena. The casket then began to ooze the same green smoke that escaped the urn earlier. Yokozuna and his men ran for cover as the image of Undertaker inside the casket mysteriously appeared on the arena's big screen. From inside, The Deadman delivered a mystical message to his assailants:

"Be not proud. The spirit of the Undertaker lives within the soul of all mankind, the eternal flame of life that cannot be extinguished, the origin of which cannot be explained. The answer lies in the everlasting spirit. Soon all mankind will witness the rebirth of the Undertaker. I will not rest in peace."

Paul Bearer held the urn high in the air as thunder reverberated throughout the pitch-black arena. Suddenly a faint light appeared over the big screen where Undertaker's body began to levitate high above the amazed crowd. The sight of The Deadman floating into the sky remains the most paranormal happening in all of WWE history and serves as a reminder that there is no destroying Undertaker.

"Soon all mankind will witness the rebirth of the Undertaker. I will not rest in peace."

CASKETS

Over the years, Undertaker has forced many unlucky souls in WWE to look death square in the eye. Locking them inside the confines of an airtight casket, The Deadman gives his victims a firsthand look of what eternity will look like for them after they take their final breath.

1991   1992

APRIL 13, 1991, *SUPERSTARS*
Undertaker slams the Ultimate Warrior inside the Funeral Parlor casket.

NOVEMBER 25, 1992, *SURVIVOR SERIES*
Undertaker stuffs Kamala inside the casket, en route to victory in WWE's first-ever pay-per-view Coffin Match, the precursor to today's Casket Match.

1992

Undertaker constructs a casket for Kamala.

1993 **1994**

JANUARY 22, 1994, *ROYAL RUMBLE*

Undertaker attempts to stuff the mighty
Yokozuna inside the casket.

NOVEMBER 23, 1994, *SURVIVOR SERIES*

Undertaker looks for revenge against Yokozuna for
his actions at the *Royal Rumble*.

Undertaker and Kama compete in a Casket Match after the *In Your House* pay-per-view went off the air in July 1995.

Undertaker regains the remnants of the urn from King Mable and Sir Mo.

JULY 23, 1995, *IN YOUR HOUSE:* THE LUMBERJACKS

DECEMBER 17, 1995, *IN YOUR HOUSE:* SEASONS BEATINGS

1995 1996

AUGUST 27, 1995, *SUMMERSLAM*

Both Undertaker and Kama tumble out of the ring and into the casket.

FEBRUARY 19, 1996, *RAW*

Diesel destroys The Deadman's casket weeks before his *WrestleMania* match against Undertaker.

Goldust picks up a shocking victory over Undertaker, thanks in large part to Mankind's interference.

MAY 28, 1996, *IN YOUR HOUSE:* *BEWARE OF DOG*

Triple H can't solve the secret of beating Undertaker at his own game.

DECEMBER 22, 1997

1997 — 1998

JULY 21, 1997

The Mastodon, Vader, finds his final resting place.

JANUARY 18, 1998, *ROYAL RUMBLE*

Shawn Michaels does everything he can to escape the casket.

Undertaker leaps over the casket onto his brother, Kane.

OCTOBER 19, 1998, *RAW*

Heidenreich learns the hard way that there's almost no beating Undertaker in a Casket Match.

JANUARY 30, 2005, *ROYAL RUMBLE*

1998   1999   2005

MAY 17, 1999, *RAW*

Undertaker, Shane McMahon, Chyna, and Triple H stand over a battered casket holding The Rock.

OCTOBER 9, 2005, *NO MERCY*

Randy and Cowboy Bob Orton celebrate their victory over Undertaker by lighting the casket holding The Phenom on fire.

Undertaker and Mark Henry do battle inside the casket.

APRIL 2, 2006, *WRESTLEMANIA 22*

Undertaker heads into battle against Chavo Guerrero.

OCTOBER 31, 2008, *SMACKDOWN*

2006 | 2008

MARCH 10, 2008, *RAW*

Undertaker enters the ring for his Casket Match against Mark Henry.

NOVEMBER 23, 2008, *SURVIVOR SERIES*

Big Show can't close the lid on Undertaker at *Survivor Series*.

THE REBIRTH

Despite promising he would not rest in peace, Undertaker remained absent for the first half of 1994, leaving many to wonder if they would ever see The Deadman again. However, as spring turned to summer a handful of people reported seeing Undertaker around their communities; but with no photographic evidence, their claims held little validity. In the end, many Undertaker fans wrote the sightings off as wishful thinking. But then, just when all hope seemed lost, Ted DiBiase revealed that he knew of The Deadman's whereabouts and later proved it by actually producing Undertaker in the flesh.

Cautiously optimistic fans appeared willing to give DiBiase the benefit of the doubt. After all, it was the Million Dollar Man who initially brought Undertaker into WWE in 1990. Paul Bearer, on the other hand, was not so easily convinced. To Bearer, seeing The Deadman fall under the tutelage of DiBiase made little sense.

Hoping to get to the bottom of what was going on, Bearer confronted DiBiase and his Undertaker on an August 1994 edition of *King's Court*. But before Bearer could prove the Million Dollar Man was up to no-good, DiBiase's Undertaker attacked the manager, grabbing him tightly by the throat. Bearer didn't stand a chance; there was no escaping the clutches of DiBiase's titan. But then, out of nowhere, the arena lights mysteriously went dark. When they came back on moments later, a freed Bearer was seen proudly proclaiming the presence of *his* Undertaker in the arena.

DiBiase continued to maintain the authenticity of his Undertaker, claiming Bearer had no proof to the contrary. That proof, however, would eventually come just days prior to *SummerSlam* when Bearer's Undertaker finally spoke after months of silence:

"Ted DiBiase, I vowed never to rest in peace. This Monday night, you bring whatever demon it is that you possess. For the time has come for the Undertaker to rise once more. Therefore, the time has come for your Undertaker to be destroyed once and for all, to rest in peace."

With that, the now-famous Undertaker versus Undertaker match was set for *SummerSlam*. DiBiase's Undertaker came to the ring first, wearing the traditional black and grey garb. Next came Paul Bearer, who was followed by druids pushing a double-wide casket believed to be holding the other Undertaker. But when the casket opened and there was no Undertaker, people began to think DiBiase may have actually been telling the truth all along.

Bearer reached deep down into the casket and pulled out an oversized urn. He then removed the lid and a preternatural light rushed from its insides. As the light shined bright in an otherwise dark arena, the shadow of an arcane figure began to slowly make its way toward the ring. When the arena lights finally went back on, the capacity crowd erupted in elation. For the first time in more than seven months, Undertaker returned!

Clad in black and purple, Bearer's Undertaker withstood everything DiBiase's man could dish out, including a Tombstone. There was no stopping The Deadman on this night. And to prove he was the real deal, Bearer's Undertaker flattened DiBiase's Deadman with an amazing three Tombstones before finally pinning him for the win.

After the match, Undertaker dumped the imposter into a ringside casket. Proving there is only one Deadman, his druids then carried the casket away and the fraud was never heard from again.

DECONSTRUCTING DIESEL

Like Harvey Wippleman before him, DiBiase refused to let the defeat of one man derail his quest to end the Undertaker. So with destruction in mind, the Million Dollar Man unleashed nearly every member of his Corporation on Undertaker, most notably King Kong Bundy, Irwin R. Schyster, and Kama. But despite having nearly endless resources, DiBiase and his crew were unable to break The Deadman.

In addition to turning back DiBiase's Million Dollar Corporation in 1995, Undertaker also earned impressive wins over the likes of Jeff Jarrett, British Bulldog, and Isaac Yankem, earning him an opportunity at Bret Hart's WWE Championship at the *Royal Rumble*. More than four years separated Undertaker from his previous reign as WWE Champion, and on this night, it appeared as though the long wait was finally over when The Deadman Tombstoned Bret Hart late in the match. When Undertaker went for the cover, however, Diesel interfered by pulling the referee from the ring, marking the end of the match and preventing The Deadman from becoming champion.

Immediately following the match, WWE President Gorilla Monsoon inexplicably named Diesel the new number one contender and announced that he would challenge the "Hit Man" for the gold at February's *In Your House*. Sensing Undertaker would almost definitely be out for revenge, the match was to be contested inside the confines of a steel cage designed to keep interfering Superstars such as The Deadman out.

Just like Undertaker the month prior, Diesel appeared to have the match in hand. With an injured Hart writhing in pain several feet away, Big Daddy Cool crawled toward the door and certain victory. Before Diesel could get to the arena floor, however, Undertaker emerged through a smoky hole in the mat and pulled the challenger down under the ring, allowing Hart to escape the cage and pick up the win.

The ongoing game of retribution ultimately resulted in Undertaker and Diesel squaring off on the grandest stage of them all, *WrestleMania XII*. With revenge on both their minds, the two nearly-seven-foot behemoths clashed as if there were no tomorrow. At one point late in the match, Diesel hit Undertaker with a pair of Jackknife powerbombs that would've assuredly ended the career of a lesser man. Undertaker simply sat up from both, proving that he is no normal man. The Deadman then put Diesel out of his misery after connecting with a Chokeslam and Tombstone for the win.

RIVAL: MANKIND

Just twenty-four hours after his grueling *WrestleMania XII* encounter with Diesel, Undertaker squared off with a young Justin Hawk Bradshaw in the main event of *Raw*. Hungry to make a name for himself, Bradshaw took a fatigued Phenom to the limits, but was ultimately unable to defeat the Undertaker. Instead, The Deadman flattened Bradshaw with a Tombstone, en route to what appeared to be a pinfall victory. Before Undertaker could cover his opponent, however, WWE newcomer Mankind ran to the ring and attacked The Deadman.

The assault was as vicious a beating as Undertaker had ever endured. Mankind nailed The Deadman with several clubbing blows before hitting him outside the ring with an elbow from the ring apron. A Mandible Claw by Mankind put an exclamation mark on the brutal beating. As *Raw* went off the air, viewers were left with the scene of a struggling Undertaker gasping for air.

Historically, Mankind's inexplicable attack on Undertaker was the first shot fired in what became one of sports-entertainment's greatest rivalries. Over the next several years, Mankind and Undertaker went on to create iconic images that took place over dozens of high-profile matches.

JUNE 23, 1996 - *KING OF THE RING*

MANKIND DEFEATED UNDERTAKER

In the weeks following Mankind's initial attack on Undertaker, the two Superstars engaged in a grim set of mind games that most notably saw the deranged newcomer pop from a casket and cost The Phenom a match with Intercontinental Champion, Goldust. When the two finally squared off at *King of the Ring*, the action was anything but pretty. Undertaker and Mankind went at each other like two pent up animals finally set free. A blatant disregard for the rules highlighted much of the match's actions. In keeping with the ongoing theme, it was the urn that ultimately brought the match to its end.

While Mankind had his Mandible Claw locked in on Undertaker, Paul Bearer snuck up behind his enemy and tried to whack him with the urn. But unfortunately for Bearer, Mankind moved at the last moment, resulting in the manager mistakenly hitting Undertaker. The force of the blow, coupled with the effects of the Mandible Claw, was enough to render The Deadman unconscious, giving the win to Mankind.

MANKIND DEFEATED UNDERTAKER IN A BOILER ROOM BRAWL

By *SummerSlam*, it had become clear that a wrestling ring could not contain the unearthly hatred Undertaker and Mankind shared. So rather than attempting to settle their score within the ropes, the two Superstars agreed to battle in a boiler room deep in the bowels of Cleveland's Gund Arena.

Undertaker opened the door to the boiler room and cautiously stepped inside, signifying the start of the match. Knowing the locale better suited Mankind's game, The Phenom carefully navigated the dark room in search of his opponent. But Mankind was nowhere to be found. Finally after several apprehensive moments, Undertaker was attacked from behind with metal piping. From the start, it was clear the Boiler Room Brawl would be anything but traditional.

After the use of some very unorthodox weaponry, including steel chains and hot furnaces, Mankind managed to escape the dreary room first; but Undertaker was not far behind. Once both Superstars made their way back to the ring, Undertaker regained the upper hand and proceeded toward what appeared to be victory. But before The Deadman could seal the deal, Paul Bearer did the unthinkable and turned on Undertaker. Fans watched in shock as Bearer whacked The Phenom with the urn, thus helping Mankind to victory.

NOVEMBER 16, 1996 –
SURVIVOR SERIES

UNDERTAKER DEFEATED MANKIND

With vengeance a top priority, Undertaker hoped to get his hands on Paul Bearer once and for all at *Survivor Series*. But first, The Phenom had to defeat Mankind in one-on-one action, per pre-match stipulations.

A caged Bearer watched from high above the ring, as Undertaker and Mankind squared off in a highly physical contest. Like their prior matches, various weapons found their way into play, including the steel steps and ringside barrier. Mankind even assaulted The Deadman with an unidentified foreign object. The attack, however, was not enough to put Undertaker away. The Phenom ultimately won the match following a Tombstone to Mankind. As a result of the win, Undertaker was awarded the opportunity to exact revenge on Bearer. But before The Deadman could open the cage, The Executioner interfered and freed the manager.

APRIL 20, 1997 - IN YOUR HOUSE: REVENGE OF THE TAKER

UNDERTAKER DEFEATED MANKIND

Fueled by a burning desire to once again manage the WWE Champion, Paul Bearer ordered Mankind to throw a fireball into the face of Undertaker in March 1997. The heinous act successfully reignited their rivalry and led to The Deadman defending his WWE Title against Mankind at *Revenge of the Taker*.

With an oversized bandage protecting his scorched right eye, Undertaker was forced to fend off an exceptionally-maniacal Mankind, who appeared more interested in further disfiguring the champ than defeating him. In the end though, an Undertaker Tombstone successfully dismissed the disturbed challenger.

After the match, Undertaker earned revenge on Paul Bearer by tossing a fireball of his own into his former manager's face, charring his pasty white skin.

OTHER NOTABLE MATCHES

October 20, 1996, *In Your House: Buried Alive:* Undertaker defeated Mankind in a Buried Alive Match.

June 28, 1998, *King of the Ring:* Undertaker defeated Mankind in a Hell in a Cell Match.

March 1, 1999, *Raw:* Mankind defeated Undertaker via countout.

UNDERTAKER VS. MANKIND

Date:	October 20, 1996
Event:	*In Your House: Buried Alive*
City:	Indianapolis, Indiana
Venue:	Market Square Arena
Commentators:	Vince McMahon, Jerry "The King" Lawler

BURIED ALIVE

After losses to Mankind at *King of the Ring* and *SummerSlam*, as well as Paul Bearer's bitter betrayal, Undertaker appeared to be in a very vulnerable position in late 1996. Never before had The Phenom been so decimated, both physically and psychologically, leaving many to wonder if he'd ever reclaim the prominence he held prior to Mankind's WWE debut. Undertaker's confidence, however, never waivered, especially heading into October's *In Your House*, where he challenged Mankind to a match that greatly played to The Deadman's strengths: A Buried Alive Match.

As the name suggests, the object of the match was to literally bury your opponent alive in a gravesite constructed inside the arena. WWE had seen dangerous matches in the past, including Steel Cage and Ladder Matches, but this contest took extreme to a whole new level. Given the perilous nature of the match, WWE had no choice but to refuse to sanction the contest. But that didn't stop Undertaker and Mankind. For them, this match was about finally destroying the other once and for all.

The match started in the ring, but soon spilled to the ringside area and into the crowd. The no-holds-barred atmosphere allowed Paul Bearer and Mankind to take liberties they wouldn't normally get away with. At one point, Bearer gave his charge an unidentifiable sharp instrument, which Mankind used to pummel Undertaker. The deranged Mankind used any blunt object within arm's reach to weaken The Phenom before delivering a double-arm DDT.

Paul Bearer gleefully predicted the end for Undertaker from ringside, but stunningly the assault failed to stop The Deadman. Instead, Undertaker sat up, showing almost no ill effects from Mankind's offense. A determined Undertaker then took a page from Mankind's playbook, nailing him with the ringside steps. Looking to finally put his nemesis away, The Phenom lifted Mankind and delivered a vicious Tombstone.

"This is worse than the Boiler Room Brawl!"

—Announcer Vince McMahon

Undertaker carried Mankind's carcass down the aisle toward the gravesite. But before The Deadman could dump him into the dirty hole, Mankind recovered and slapped on his patented Mandible Claw. The end appeared near for Undertaker. Just to make sure, however, Mankind attempted to hit The Phenom with the urn. The attack never landed. Instead, Undertaker miraculously sat up and grabbed Mankind by the neck before ultimately Chokeslamming his rival right down to the bottom of the grave.

A motionless Mankind lay at the base of the tomb, while Undertaker covered him with shovelfuls of dirt, signifying the end of the match. Finally, The Deadman had gained retribution from Mankind after months of torment. But simply earning the win wasn't enough for Undertaker. He continued to bury Mankind with dirt. WWE Officials rushed to Mankind's aid, but a focused Phenom merely tossed them away. There was no stopping Undertaker.

Before Undertaker could finish the job, a mysterious masked man snuck up from behind and clobbered him with a shovel. By this time, Mankind had recovered and climbed out of the grave. Together, the mystery man and Mankind dumped The Deadman into the grave and began to cover *him* with dirt. Making matters worse for Undertaker, Mankind and his accomplice were soon joined by Justin Hawk Bradshaw, Hunter Hearst-Helmsley, Crush, and Goldust.

"Undertaker's gone forever," Paul Bearer joyfully yelled, as the six Superstars completed covering The Phenom with six feet of dirt, making it impossible for him to breathe. The situation was undeniably grim for Undertaker. But just as Mankind and company were about to celebrate, thunder and lightning overcame the arena, sending the Superstars running in fear.

As the paranormal activity continued, the inconceivable happened when Undertaker's hand emerged from under the mound of dirt. Against all odds, The Deadman refused to be buried, and as *In Your House* went off the air, Vince McMahon could be heard proclaiming loudly, "He's alive! The Undertaker's alive! The Undertaker lives!"

REGAINING THE GOLD

When Mankind proved unable to destroy Undertaker, Paul Bearer turned to the mysterious masked man who helped temporarily bury The Deadman at *In Your House: Buried Alive*. Hailing from Parts Unknown and identified simply as The Executioner, Paul Bearer's man was three hundred pounds of pure destruction. But despite The Executioner's savage disposition, he too was unable to stop Undertaker when the two squared off in an Armageddon Rules Match at *In Your House: It's Time*.

Following The Executioner's loss, a desperate Paul Bearer tapped Vader to be the next in his long line of Superstars eager to finish Undertaker. The move nearly worked. At the 1997 *Royal Rumble*, with a little help from an interfering Bearer, Vader actually did defeat The Phenom. Still, the loss did little to unnerve Undertaker. Instead, following the defeat, The Deadman proved to be as devastating as ever and was awarded an opportunity at Sycho Sid's WWE Championship at *WrestleMania 13*.

LUCKY NUMBER 13

Undertaker's famed *WrestleMania* undefeated streak certainly wasn't a topic of conversation heading into the thirteenth annual crown jewel of sports-entertainment. But with a 5-0 record, and three of those wins coming against future WWE Hall of Famers, it was hard to deny that The Deadman had a knack for coming up big on the biggest stage of them all. This night proved to be no different.

WrestleMania 13 marked the first-ever *WrestleMania* main event for Undertaker. To commemorate the occasion, The Deadman competed in his original black and grey gear, something he hadn't done since 1994. Longtime Undertaker supporters were thrilled to see the traditional colors return. But unfortunately for The Phenom, the black and grey did little to help him get an early advantage on Sid. Instead, the champ controlled much of the match's initial moments with a focused attack on Undertaker's lower back.

Sid's simple strategy of targeting the lumbar region worked to perfection. It wasn't until he deviated from that game plan and climbed to the top rope that trouble arose. Realizing Sid was out of his element, Undertaker grabbed the unsteady champion and slammed him to the mat. From there, The Deadman nailed Sid with a top rope clothesline. The end appeared to be near. Undertaker scooped Sid up for the Tombstone, but somehow, the champ was able to reverse it and nail The Phenom with his own signature move. Sid confidently crossed Undertaker's arms over his chest and went for the arrogant cover. But The Deadman refused to lose to his own move, kicking out at two.

The capacity crowd rose to its feet realizing they were witnessing one of the year's best matches. Unfortunately, though, the amazing action was soon marred by controversy when Bret Hart interfered in the contest, not once but twice. Both attacks were aimed at Sid, with the final one proving to be fatal to the champion's reign. Standing at the ring apron, the "Hit Man" grabbed Sid's head and drove his neck down over the top rope. The impact dazed the champ, who inadvertently staggered right into the arms of Undertaker, who picked Sid up and flattened him with a Tombstone for the win.

HEARTBREAK

For the first time in more than five years, Undertaker was once again WWE Champion. Over the next several months, The Deadman made up for lost time, defeating all challengers in convincing fashion. Stone Cold Steve Austin. Faarooq. Mankind. Vader. They all tried to end Undertaker's reign atop WWE, but each and every one of them fell victim to the Tombstone. It wasn't until The Phenom's *SummerSlam* match with Bret Hart and some very questionable officiating that Undertaker's reign was put in serious jeopardy.

Heading into the match, the anti-American Hart arrogantly vowed to never compete in the United States again if he wasn't successful in his quest to capture Undertaker's WWE Championship. As the match drew closer, however, Hart's confidence dwindled when it was announced that Shawn Michaels would serve as the match's special guest referee. Going up against the dominant Undertaker would be hard enough; adding longtime rival HBK to the mix would make it nearly impossible, the "Hit Man" thought.

Luckily for Hart, Michaels made a similar vow heading into *SummerSlam*: If he failed to call the action down the middle, he too would no longer compete on American soil. With that, Hart's chances of victory increased dramatically. In fact, it was that promise from HBK that ultimately lead to Undertaker's undoing.

Late in the match while Michaels was preoccupied outside of the ring, Hart blindsided The Deadman. Once back in the ring, HBK saw the evidence of Hart's attack and accused the "Hit Man" of wrongdoing. Hart not only denied the allegation, but also spat in Michaels's face in the process. Furious with being covered in spit, HBK took the foreign object and viciously swung it at the "Hit Man." Hart, however, moved out of the way at the last moment, causing HBK to connect with Undertaker instead.

As Hart went for the cover, Michaels's promise to call the action down the middle raced through his head. In a matter of mere seconds, HBK had to decide if he was going to count Undertaker's shoulders to the mat or break his vow and thus never compete in the United States again. In the end, Michaels held true to his word and made the three count. Bret Hart had won the WWE Championship, despite HBK being the one to take The Deadman down.

The loss effectively ended Undertaker's four-plus month reign atop sports-entertainment, the longest of his four WWE Championship reigns. It also kicked off a historic rivalry with Shawn Michaels, one that resulted in the debut of two WWE icons: Hell in a Cell and Kane!

UNDERTAKER VS. SHAWN MICHAELS

HELL IN A CELL

Date:	October 5, 1997
Event:	*In Your House: Badd Blood*
City:	St. Louis, Missouri
Venue:	Kiel Center
Commentators:	Vince McMahon, Jim Ross, Jerry "The King" Lawler

After witnessing their beloved Shawn Michaels cost Undertaker the WWE Championship at *SummerSlam*, many fans assumed HBK's actions were nothing more than an unfortunate mistake. But those who elected to support Michaels quickly had their theory discredited when HBK followed *SummerSlam* with a months-long assault aimed at annihilating The Deadman.

Joining Michaels in his ongoing campaign against the Undertaker were his D-Generation X cohorts, Triple H, Chyna, and Rick Rude. As would eventually become the norm in the years that followed, the newly-formed DX used its numbers advantage to out-muscle The Phenom at every turn, leaving many to wonder if Undertaker would ever find success in his battle against HBK. Luckily for The Deadman, however, a WWE first would finally give him the opportunity to square off against Michaels sans any outside interference.

At *Badd Blood* in October 1997, Undertaker and HBK competed in WWE's first-ever Hell in a Cell match. With more than one ton of steel surrounding the entirety of the ring, there was no way DX could weasel their way into this encounter, making The Phenom the heavy favorite going in. And once the bell rang, Michaels knew he was in big trouble.

HBK's signature conceit was conspicuously absent as he circled the ring hoping to steer clear of the Undertaker's wrath. But there was no escaping The Deadman on this night. Eventually, Undertaker caught HBK with a Big Boot, followed by the pugnacious attack of a man unleashing months of pent-up frustration. Seeking safety, a battered and desperate HBK eventually climbed the Cell's inner walls, hoping the heights would keep The Phenom away—but they couldn't. In fact, scurrying up the Cell eventually did more harm than good for Michaels, who was viciously jerked from the wall onto the hard arena floor.

Amazingly, HBK showed flashes of offense throughout the match, including piledriving Undertaker onto the steel ring steps. But despite these moments of light, Michaels displayed little confidence in himself and looked to hightail it at the first possible opening.

With a ringside cameraman downed by an attack at the hands of HBK, Commissioner Sgt. Slaughter had no choice but to open the Cell and allow EMTs to tend to the fallen worker. Once the door was open, though, Michaels darted out of the Cell and toward the back. Little did HBK

realize that he may have been safer *inside* the confines of Hell in a Cell. A determined Undertaker soon caught up with Michaels and delivered an even greater beating on the outside of the cage, including spearing him face first into the steel.

Seeking that elusive safe haven, HBK climbed to the top of the Cell in what would turn out to be another imprudent decision. Undertaker quickly followed Michaels atop the structure, where he continued his merciless assault. Realizing the top of the Cell was a bad idea, HBK attempted to climb down its side, but the ongoing theme remained the same: There was no freedom from The Phenom. Undertaker kicked Michaels's hands from the cage, sending him sailing through the air, as well as through the Spanish announce table.

With the end near, Undertaker dragged his prey back inside the ring where he could officially end the onslaught. But before The Deadman could be awarded the victory, the arena lights mysteriously went dark and Paul Bearer emerged from the back with a mountainous masked man fans could only assume was Kane.

"That's gotta be...That's gotta be Kane!"

—Announcer Vince McMahon

Kane tore the door off the Cell, climbed in the ring, and looked his older brother in the eye for the first time in years. Thinking Kane was dead, Undertaker simply stared at him in complete disbelief. And before he could truly assess the situation, The Phenom found himself on the receiving end of a Tombstone at the hands of his own flesh and blood. Satisfied with his actions, Kane exited the ring, as a ravaged HBK crawled atop Undertaker and picked up the win.

"Kane has defeated the Undertaker. But in the record book, it will have a victory for Michaels."

—Vince McMahon

HE'S ALIVE!

When Undertaker set Paul Bearer's face ablaze at *In Your House: Revenge of the Taker*, the manager couldn't help but be reminded of an eerily similar event that occurred twenty years earlier. According to Bearer, the incident was so horrific and damning to Undertaker that neither he nor The Deadman ever spoke a word of it to anybody within WWE. But after having his face charred at the hands of Undertaker, Bearer threatened to finally reveal the harrowing secret. The only way the manager would agree to keep the matter under wraps was if The Phenom agreed to come back home and once again fall under Bearer's tutelage.

A conflicted Undertaker struggled with whether to succumb to Bearer's blackmail. He clearly didn't want his past publicized, but neither did he have a desire to reunite with the ultimate betrayer. In the end, though, The Deadman ultimately decided that his secret was too great to uncover and gave in to Bearer's managerial demand.

Over the next few weeks, including Undertaker's main event match against Faarooq at *King of the Ring*, Paul Bearer was back at The Phenom's side. Only this time, the manager used every opening he could to berate Undertaker and remind him that he held a powerful secret over his head. Eventually, being mistreated and humiliated in public became too much to take for The Deadman, who finally broke free from Bearer, regardless of the consequences.

Left with no other choice, Paul Bearer used a *Raw* interview with Vince McMahon as his platform to reveal The Phenom's horrible secret. But before simply blurting it out, the manager painted a beautiful picture of a little funeral home that sat on a hill two decades prior. It was a family-run funeral home, owned by Undertaker's father, who was also Bearer's mentor at the time. One afternoon while on his way out, Bearer noticed Undertaker and his impressionable younger brother, Kane, sneaking behind the garage with cigarettes and chemicals from the embalming room. When Bearer returned hours later, he was met by fire trucks, ambulances, smoke, and steam.

The funeral home had been reduced to a pile of ashes. Inside were Undertaker's parents and younger brother. The only one presumably not claimed by the fire was the young Undertaker, who Paul Bearer noticed hiding in nearby bushes as medical professionals dragged his family's lifeless bodies from the blaze.

"Undertaker, you burnt the funeral home to the ground," Paul Bearer exclaimed before revealing an even greater secret, a secret that not even The Deadman knew. According to Bearer, the young brother Undertaker believed was killed in the fire was actually still alive. He was disfigured and considerably traumatized, but very much alive.

"He's alive! Kane is alive, Undertaker. He's breathing!"
—Paul Bearer

FACING DEATH

Undertaker spent much of the summer and fall of 1997 listening to Paul Bearer call him a murderer. But despite the grave claims, The Phenom did his best to put his past behind him and march forward with his WWE career. Part of moving forward meant agreeing to face Shawn Michaels in WWE's first-ever Hell in a Cell match at *In Your House: Badd Blood*. During the match, however, putting his past behind him proved impossible for Undertaker, who was shockingly confronted mid-match with the brother he once believed to be dead, Kane.

Not only did Kane's appearance at *Badd Blood* cost Undertaker his match against Michaels, but it also served as the launching point for a vicious assault on the WWE roster at the hands of the Big Red Monster. Among the first poor souls to be victimized were Matt and Jeff Hardy, as well as Flash Funk. And with each passing attack, Paul Bearer reminded the entire world that Kane would destroy all of WWE until he got to Undertaker.

Hoping his words would somehow stop his brother's senseless attacks, Undertaker finally decided to tell his side of the story in October 1997. Shockingly, The Phenom corroborated much of Bearer's version of the events that happened twenty years earlier. However, there was one very key difference in Undertaker's version. Instead of The Deadman being the one that set the fire, Undertaker claimed that while he was off doing chores, it was actually Kane who set the funeral home ablaze.

Undertaker showed never-before-seen emotions while continuing his story. In the days that followed his family's death, The Deadman said, Paul Bearer took him to the neighboring funeral home to see the charred remains of his deceased mother lying on a cold steel table. Being as young as he was at the time, Undertaker's natural inclination was to look away. But Bearer insisted that the small boy take in the severity of the situation; he demanded Undertaker stare at the dead body of the woman who raised him.

That day changed Undertaker forever. From that moment forward, The Phenom began to draw strength from the spirit of the dead, particularly the spirits of his fallen family. But while Undertaker was fueled by the hatred he had for Paul Bearer, he refused to battle his own flesh and blood, Kane. Even when Kane attacked Undertaker in the weeks that followed, The Deadman remained steadfast in his claim that he would never battle blood.

Undertaker stayed true to his word, and even took it a step further in December 1997, when he helped his brother fend off an attack at the hands of several Superstars, including Flash Funk, the Disciples of Apocalypse, and the Headbangers. At that point, it became clear that an Undertaker versus Kane match would never happen. So rather than continuing to goad his older brother, the Big Red Monster actually returned Undertaker's earlier favor and helped him fend off an attack against D-Generation X. Finally, after months of being at odds, it appeared Undertaker and Kane were at long last on the same page.

Unfortunately for Undertaker, however, Kane's olive branch was nothing more than a smoke screen. While The Deadman was competing against Shawn Michaels in a Casket Match at the 1998 *Royal Rumble*, Kane hit the ring to seemingly help Undertaker, who had become unfairly outmanned by the interfering New Age Outlaws and Los Boricuas. But rather than help his brother, Kane Chokeslammed Undertaker into the casket, marking the end of the match, as well as their supposed union.

While Undertaker tried to recuperate inside, Kane and Paul Bearer padlocked the casket, giving The Deadman no exit. The devious duo then did the unthinkable. With Undertaker locked inside, Kane poured gasoline atop the casket before ultimately sending it up in flames with The Phenom inside.

Kane and Paul Bearer rejoiced as the *Royal Rumble* went off the air, while fans everywhere questioned if they'd ever see Undertaker again.

UNDERTAKER VS. KANE

Date:	March 29, 1998
Event:	*WrestleMania XIV*
City:	Boston, Massachusetts
Venue:	FleetCenter
Commentators:	Jim Ross, Jerry "The King" Lawler
Special ring announcer:	Pete Rose

As the weeks turned to months and there was still no sign of Undertaker, distressed fans were forced to accept the fact that Kane's fiery attack at the *Royal Rumble* may have actually succeeded in eradicating The Deadman from WWE. And to put the final nail in the coffin that symbolized any potential return, Paul Bearer conducted a memorial ceremony for Undertaker in March 1998, complete with a ten-bell salute.

Once the bells stopped ringing, however, Kane and Paul Bearer were confronted by their worst nightmare. Out of nowhere a lightning bolt struck a nearby casket, breaking it to pieces. Inside was The Deadman, who had some very pointed words for his ineffective executioners: "Welcome to hell and the demon who will lead you into eternal damnation. Kane, you disappointed me. Is that the best effort that you could put together at the *Royal Rumble*? Did you think that could destroy me? Don't you know that you cannot destroy that which does not wish to perish? And you, Paul, the audacity to come out here, week after week, and claim responsibility for my disappearance. The fact of the matter is, on those times when I return to the world of darkness, it's of my own accord. It's a time for spiritual healing. It's a time for the truth and I know the truth.

"And this trip, what I was doing was soothing the souls of my parents because I had to explain to them why I would have to do the one thing I promised never to do. I will walk straight through the fires of hell to face you, Kane. And when you look into the eyes of your older brother, you will understand why I am the most feared entity in WWE. You will understand why I am the reaper of wayward souls; and you will understand why I am the Lord of Darkness.

"Kane, there is one thought that I want you to think about between now and *WrestleMania XIV*, March 29th. I want you to remember when we were small children and we would begin to fight; mother and father were always there to pull me off of you. Well, this time, there won't be anyone to save you. May the hounds of hell eat your rotting soul. And you will rest in peace!"

With that, Undertaker's longtime pledge to never battle his own flesh and blood was shattered, and at *WrestleMania XIV*, two brothers born of the same blood would finally square off in one of the most anticipated matches in recent WWE history.

Undertaker tried to control much of the match's early-going, but unlike most Deadman contests of the past, his offense had no effect on Kane. As a result, the Big Red Monster was able to manhandle Undertaker in a way nobody had ever seen before.

> ## "Did you think that could destroy me? Don't you know that you cannot destroy that which does not wish to perish?"
>
> —Undertaker

Kane intensified his onslaught when the action managed to spill out to the arena floor. Employing a methodical and deliberate approach, the Big Red Machine targeted Undertaker's back and ribs utilizing the oversized steel ring steps. Paul Bearer even got into the game, kicking his former protégé while he was down.

Back on the inside, Kane looked to put his brother away with a Tombstone, but despite being dismantled throughout much of the match, Undertaker miraculously kicked out. Upon returning to his feet, it appeared the Lord of Darkness was breathing new life and would stop at nothing to put his brother down. Looking for the win, Undertaker nailed Kane with a Tombstone and went for the cover. But somehow, the Big Red Monster managed to kick out at two. Unfazed, The Deadman simply delivered a second Tombstone, but this one proved to be equally ineffective. At this point, it was clear that Undertaker wasn't dealing with an average man. Determined to put his brother away once and for all, Undertaker flattened Kane with a *third* Tombstone. Unlike the others, this one did the trick, as The Phenom was able to pick up the pinfall victory.

The win went a long way toward Undertaker proving his dominance over his brother, Kane, while also extending The Deadman's undefeated *WrestleMania* streak to seven straight.

ENTER THE DEADMAN

April 4, 1993, *WrestleMania IX*: Undertaker vs. Giant Gonzales

April 2, 1995, *WrestleMania XI*: Undertaker vs. King Kong Bundy

Aside from the chill overtaking the arena, Undertaker's earliest entrances were not all that different than those of other Superstars of the early 1990s. But over the years, just as Undertaker has, The Deadman's entrance has evolved into a spectacle unlike anything ever witnessed in WWE: complete with ominous thunder, scorching fire, and mysterious druids leading the way.

November 17, 1996, *Survivor Series*: Undertaker vs. Mankind

February 24, 1997, *Raw:* Undertaker vs. Faarooq

April 28, 1997, *Raw:* Undertaker vs. British Bulldog

March 29, 1998,
WrestleMania XIV:
Undertaker vs. Kane

March 28, 1999, *WrestleMania XV*: Undertaker vs. Big Boss Man

April 28, 1997, *Raw*: Undertaker vs. British Bulldog

August 22, 1999, *SummerSlam*: Undertaker & Big Show vs. Kane & X-Pac

May 21, 2000, *Judgment Day*: Triple H vs. The Rock (with interference from Undertaker)

May 25, 2000, *SmackDown*: Undertaker vs. Shane McMahon

March 14, 2004, *WrestleMania XX*: Undertaker vs. Kane

March 30, 2008, *WrestleMania XXIV*: Undertaker vs. Edge

March 28, 2010, *WrestleMania XXVI*: Undertaker vs. Shawn Michaels

April 3, 2011, *WrestleMania XXVII*: Undertaker vs. Triple H

April 7, 2013, *WrestleMania XXIX*: Undertaker vs. CM Punk

"I'LL MAKE YOU FAMOUS"

MATCHES UNDERTAKER PUT ON THE MAP*

*WINNERS IN BOLD

INFERNO MATCH

A contest concocted by the evil mind of Paul Bearer, the Inferno Match requires its combatants do battle in a ring surrounded by walls of fire. The only way to win is to set your opponent ablaze, which is exactly what Undertaker did to Kane in WWE's first two Inferno Matches.

1. **Undertaker** vs. Kane, *In Your House: Unforgiven*, April 26, 1998

2. **Undertaker** vs. Kane, *Raw*, February 22, 1999

HELL IN A CELL

With tons of steel surrounding the entirety of the ring, Hell in Cell not only eliminates the possibility of outside interference, it also guarantees its competitors are put through one of the most grueling matches of their careers. Over the years, no Superstar in history has competed in as many Hell in a Cell Matches as Undertaker.

1. Undertaker vs. **Shawn Michaels**, *In Your House: Badd Blood*, October 5, 1997

2. Undertaker & Stone Cold Steve Austin vs. Kane & Mankind, *Raw*, June 15, 1998 (no contest)

3. **Undertaker** vs. Mankind, *King of the Ring*, June 28, 1998

4. **Undertaker** vs. Big Boss Man, *WrestleMania XV*, March 28, 1999

5. Undertaker vs. The Rock vs. Triple H vs. Rikishi vs. Stone Cold Steve Austin vs. **Kurt Angle**, *Armageddon*, December 10, 2000

6. Undertaker vs. **Brock Lesnar**, *No Mercy*, October 20, 2002

7. **Undertaker** vs. Randy Orton, *Armageddon*, December 18, 2005

8. Undertaker vs. **Batista**, *Survivor Series*, November 18, 2007

9. **Undertaker** vs. Edge, *SummerSlam*, August 17, 2008

10. **Undertaker** vs. CM Punk, *Hell in a Cell*, October 4, 2009

11. Undertaker vs. **Kane**, *Hell in a Cell*, October 3, 2010

12. **Undertaker** vs. Triple H, *WrestleMania XXVIII*, April 1, 2012

CASKET MATCH

Introduced to WWE by Undertaker in 1992, the Casket Match (then known as the Coffin Match) forces competitors to confront their worst fear: Death. And the only way to succeed in a Casket Match is to put your opposition inside the cold, dark casket and close the lid.

1. **Undertaker** vs. Kamala, *Survivor Series*, November 24, 1992

2. Undertaker vs. **Yokozuna**, *Royal Rumble*, January 22, 1994

3. **Undertaker** vs. Yokozuna, *Survivor Series*, November 23, 1994

4. **Undertaker** vs. Kama, *In Your House*, July 23, 1995

5. **Undertaker** vs. Kama, *SummerSlam*, August 27, 1995

6. **Undertaker** vs. Mabel, *In Your House*, December 17, 1995

7. Undertaker vs. **Goldust**, *In Your House*, May 26, 1996

8. Undertaker vs. **Vader**, Live Event, March 16, 1997

9. Undertaker vs. **Shawn Michaels**, *Royal Rumble*, January 18, 1998

10. Undertaker vs. Kane, *Raw*, October 19, 1998 (no contest)

11. **Undertaker** vs. The Rock, *Raw*, May 17, 1999

12. **Undertaker** vs. Heidenreich, *Royal Rumble*, January 30, 2005

13. Undertaker vs. **"Cowboy" Bob & Randy Orton**, *No Mercy*, October 9, 2005

14. **Undertaker** vs. Mark Henry, *WrestleMania 22*, April 2, 2006

15. **Undertaker** vs. Mark Henry, *Raw*, March 10, 2008

16. **Undertaker** vs. Chavo Guerrero, *SmackDown*, October 31, 2008

17. **Undertaker** vs. Big Show, *Survivor Series*, November 23, 2008

BURIED ALIVE MATCH

As the name suggests, a Buried Alive Match requires a Superstar to literally bury his opponent in a grave with mounds of dirt to be declared the winner. With five Buried Alive Matches to his credit, Undertaker has become synonymous with the blood-curdling contest.

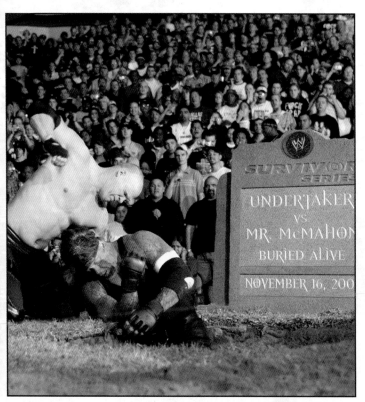

1. **Undertaker** vs. Mankind, *In Your House: Buried Alive*, October 20, 1996

2. Undertaker vs. **Stone Cold Steve Austin**, *In Your House: Rock Bottom*, December 13, 1998

3. **Undertaker & Big Show** vs. Rock 'n' Sock Connection, *SmackDown*, September, 9, 1999

4. Undertaker vs. **Mr. McMahon**, *Survivor Series*, November 16, 2003

5. Undertaker vs. **Kane**, *Bragging Rights*, October 24, 2010

LAST RIDE MATCH

No disqualifications. No countouts. No pinfalls. No submissions. The only way to win the morbid Last Ride Match is to stuff your opponent into the back of a hearse and have it drive out of the arena.

1. Undertaker vs. **JBL**, *No Mercy*, October 3, 2004

2. **Undertaker** vs. Mr. Kennedy, *Armageddon*, December 17, 2006

UNDERTAKER VS. MANKIND

Date:	June 28, 1998
Event:	*King of the Ring*
City:	Pittsburgh, Pennsylvania
Venue:	Civic Arena
Commentators:	Jim Ross, Jerry "The King" Lawler

HELL IN A CELL

With very little Hell in a Cell history to draw upon, nobody really knew what to expect when Undertaker and Mankind squared off inside the ominous structure at the 1998 *King of the Ring*. The only absolute certainty was that anything could happen. But despite preparing for unpredictability, nobody ever envisioned the match would actually start *atop* the Cell, as opposed to within it.

But that's exactly what happened when Mankind climbed the Cell during his introduction and awaited Undertaker. Not to be outdone, The Deadman followed Mankind to the top of the structure where the action immediately kicked off at a fevered pace. Lighting quick punches were exchanged from high above the arena floor when seemingly out of nowhere, Undertaker dragged Mankind to the edge and forcefully threw him clear off the Cell and through the Spanish announce table below.

"Good God almighty, good God almighty, they've killed him!" screamed announcer Jim Ross, as Mankind lay a broken mess under the remains of the announce table.

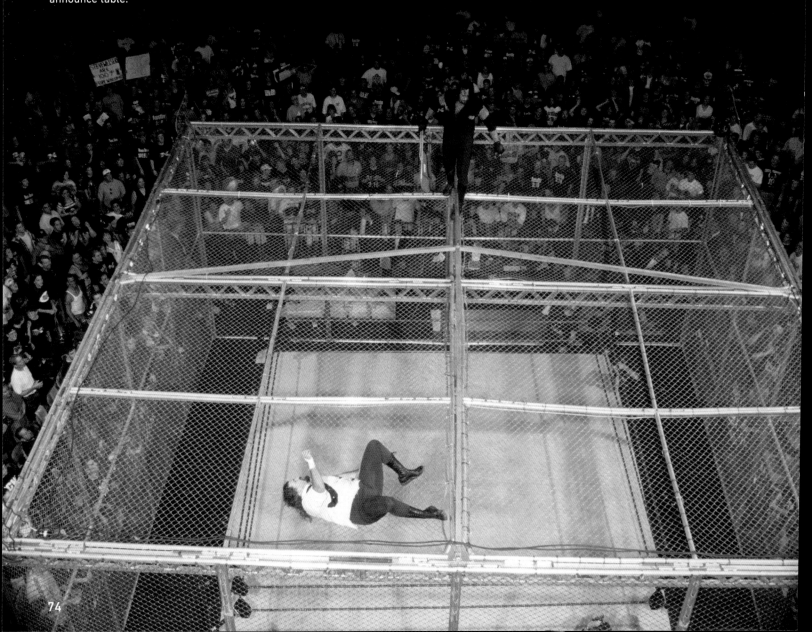

"Good God almighty, good God almighty, they've killed him!"

—Announcer Jim Ross

"With God as my witness, he is broken in half," continued Ross, as Vince McMahon, Terry Funk, Syl. Slaughter, and a whole host of WWE officials and doctors tended to a motionless Mankind. Paramedics were finally able to get Mankind on a stretcher and wheel him toward the back. But before they could reach their desired destination, Mankind miraculously pulled his battered body from the stretcher and began to drag his near lifeless frame back toward the Cell. And just like he did before, The Deranged One went straight to the top of the structure.

Unfortunately for Mankind, his second stint atop the Cell didn't end much better. Within moments of reaching the top, Mankind found himself in the clutches of an Undertaker Chokeslam. With all his energy, The Phenom hoisted his opponent high in the air and drove him down through the Cell's top and onto the unforgiving mat more than a dozen feet below.

The vicious attack would've ended a mere mortal, but on this night, Mankind appeared indestructible. After absorbing arguably the two most brutal blows in WWE history, Mankind somehow raged on. And he did so with a smile, as he poured hundreds of thumbtacks onto the ring's mat.

In the end, the introduction of thumbtacks proved to be a poor decision for Mankind, who found himself both backdropped and Chokeslammed onto the diminutive weapons. Undertaker then scooped up the human pincushion for a Tombstone and the win, finally putting Mankind out of his misery.

"This has been the most ungodly match that I think perhaps we will ever see."

—Announcer Jim Ross

BROTHERS OF DESTRUCTION

Undertaker's defeat of Kane at *WrestleMania XIV* was meant to be the defining moment for The Deadman in his ongoing battle against his brother. But when the Big Red Monster viciously attacked The Phenom after the match, it became clear that the Undertaker-Kane saga was far from over. In the months that followed, everything WWE fans believed to be real was flipped upside down, and a wicked truth was revealed that would forever change the way the world looked at Undertaker.

In a bit of retribution from the fiery events of the Royal Rumble, Undertaker returned the favor when he set Kane ablaze in an Inferno Match at *Unforgiven 1998*. And while the sight of The Deadman setting his own flesh and blood on fire was peculiar enough, amazingly the story became even more odd weeks later when Paul Bearer claimed he was Kane's father.

"I came through the door and she took me right there," recalled Bearer, referring to the night Kane was conceived on the kitchen floor of the family's funeral home. According to Bearer, he hadn't planned on having an affair with Undertaker's mother. But her revealing lingerie, coupled with the few beers he had that night, made it nearly impossible for the nineteen-year-old virgin to resist his first romantic tryst.

After DNA tests supported Bearer's claim, Undertaker and Kane slowly began to revive their bond that had been dead for twenty years. Given what the duo had gone through over the prior several months, many were skeptical to see the brothers operate on the same page, while others were flat-out in denial of their reunion. Regardless, the unorthodox pairing didn't stop Mr. McMahon from using Undertaker and Kane as pawns in his quest to topple his heated rival, Stone Cold Steve Austin.

Tired of having Stone Cold represent his WWE as its champion, McMahon came up with a master plan to have Austin defend the title against both Undertaker and Kane in a Triple Threat Match at Breakdown. And to ensure Stone Cold received the brunt of the match's assault, McMahon declared that neither Undertaker nor Kane could pin each other, meaning they both would target Austin throughout the match.

McMahon's plan worked brilliantly—almost too brilliantly. As expected, Undertaker and Kane did, in fact, beat Stone Cold mercilessly. But when it came time to pin the champ for the win, both Superstars went for the cover, making both Undertaker and Kane winners of the match.

The controversial outcome resulted in the WWE Championship being vacated, which partially satisfied Mr. McMahon. For the boss, there was joy in Stone Cold no longer being WWE Champion. But McMahon wanted more; he wanted to humiliate Austin, so he ordered The Texas Rattlesnake to officiate the Undertaker versus Kane match that would crown a new champion at *Judgment Day*. That way, Austin would be forced to stand in the middle of the ring and raise the hand of the new champion.

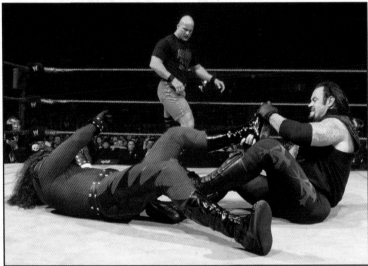

In typical Stone Cold fashion, Austin refused to play by the rules, and instead of actually naming a true winner of the match, The Texas Rattlesnake counted the shoulders of both Undertaker and Kane down before ultimately declaring himself the winner. The antics didn't sit well with Mr. McMahon, who fired Austin on the spot. But perhaps even more surprising than Stone Cold defying the boss was the Undertaker-Kane-Paul Bearer interaction that occurred toward the end of the match and in the hours that followed.

Just when it looked like Kane was going to put Undertaker away once and for all, Paul Bearer entered the ring with a foreign object and pleaded with his son to let him be the one to finally knock The Deadman out of commission. Kane acquiesced to his father's request, which ultimately proved costly. Rather than nailing Undertaker, Bearer whacked his own son, knocking him unconscious.

Bearer's betrayal of Kane not only ended the strong father-son dynamic that had been running roughshod over WWE for months, but it also marked the shocking reunion of Undertaker and Paul Bearer. After years of being estranged, the dark duo was finally back together again. This time, though, they were more evil than ever before. Perhaps their most diabolic act came one night after *Judgment Day* when they verbally assaulted Kane for being stupid and weak. Then, just when it seemed things couldn't get any worse for Kane, Undertaker remorselessly confessed to setting the fire that killed his parents and mentally and physically scarred his brother.

Never before had Undertaker shown such a callous side. And as the words carelessly left his mouth, it became painfully clear that the Undertaker of old was gone, and in his place was one of the most evil presences WWE had ever seen.

RIVAL: STONE COLD STEVE AUSTIN

When Undertaker knocked Kane unconscious at *Judgment Day*, The Deadman assumed he was mere moments away from another WWE Championship reign. But unfortunately for Undertaker, that reign never came, thanks to special guest referee Stone Cold Steve Austin refusing to make the three count.

Furious over not becoming WWE Champion, Undertaker vowed to unleash an evil plague on WWE. And he planned on starting with the man he blamed for not becoming champion: Stone Cold.

Driven by malevolent intentions, Undertaker stayed true to his word when he viciously assaulted Austin with a steel shovel. As a result of the attack, Stone Cold was forced to seek aid at a nearby medical facility. Ironically, though, The Texas Rattlesnake found himself in even more trouble once there, as Undertaker kidnapped the ailing Austin and drove away with him in the back of a hearse.

The Deadman took Stone Cold to a graveyard, where he planned on burying Austin alive. But midway through, Undertaker had a change of heart and instead decided to embalm Stone Cold while he was still breathing. Luckily for Austin, Kane stepped in before The Phenom and Paul Bearer could begin the embalming process. On this night, Austin was able to find freedom from Undertaker's sadistic plan, and at *In Your House: Rock Bottom*, The Texas Rattlesnake planned on returning the favor by burying the Lord of Darkness alive.

DECEMBER 13, 1998 – IN YOUR HOUSE: ROCK BOTTOM

STONE COLD STEVE AUSTIN DEFEATED UNDERTAKER IN A BURIED ALIVE MATCH

After being strapped to the Undertaker symbol one week earlier, Stone Cold entered *Rock Bottom* more furious than ever, and wasted little time unleashing his emotions on the Lord of Darkness well before the opening bell even rang. Looking to end it early, Austin dragged Undertaker to the gravesite, where the action continued for several more minutes.

Unlike a traditional match, much of the battle occurred outside the ring and included a slew of unorthodox items such as the ringside barrier, shovels, and even steel gas containers. In fact, it was these containers that eventually spelled the end for Undertaker. While atop the giant mound of dirt, Austin nailed The Deadman with the gas container twice before finally flattening him with a Stunner. Eyeing victory, The Rattlesnake dumped Undertaker into the grave; but before he could finish the job, Austin inexplicably chased Paul Bearer to the back.

With Stone Cold out of the picture, Undertaker was eventually able to climb out of the grave. But once he did, a giant explosion occurred inside the burial site and from the grave emerged Kane. The Big Red Monster Tombstoned a battered Undertaker and rolled him back into the gaping dirt hole.

After a Stunner and Tombstone, it was clear that the end was near for The Deadman. But just to make sure, Stone Cold reemerged from the back with a backhoe, which he used to cover Undertaker with hundreds of pounds of cold, wet dirt for the win.

MAY 23, 1999 - *OVER THE EDGE*

UNDERTAKER DEFEATED STONE COLD STEVE AUSTIN FOR THE WWE CHAMPIONSHIP

Utilizing the power that comes with the McMahon surname, Shane McMahon concocted a diabolical plan that put Steve Austin's WWE Championship reign in seemingly insurmountable jeopardy when he named himself the special guest referee heading into *Over the Edge*. The blatant miscarriage of justice didn't sit well with WWE Commissioner Shawn Michaels, who responded by announcing Mr. McMahon would serve as referee in the match. But Shane proved to be one step ahead of HBK when he had his Corporate Ministry brutally attack his father prior to the match, thus making the elder McMahon unable to officiate.

As expected, Shane McMahon did everything in his power to ensure Stone Cold did not leave *Over the Edge* with the WWE Championship, including blatantly refusing to count when Undertaker's shoulders were clearly down for the three count. Having seen enough, a battered Mr. McMahon hobbled to the ring in an attempt to right the wrongs of his dishonorable son. But Shane again remained one step ahead of his father, attacking him before he could declare Austin the winner.

Realizing he had to work fast now that his father had interjected himself, Shane purposefully bumped Undertaker atop Stone Cold and made potentially the fastest three count in WWE history. As a result of the underhanded officiating, Undertaker walked away with the win and his third WWE Championship reign.

JULY 25, 1999 – FULLY LOADED

WWE CHAMPION STONE COLD STEVE AUSTIN DEFEATED UNDERTAKER IN A FIRST BLOOD MATCH

When Undertaker lost the WWE Championship to Stone Cold in June 1999, the Lord of Darkness immediately responded by busting the new champ open in a vicious post-match beat down. The crimson mask that covered Austin's face made it painfully clear that The Deadman was not done with The Rattlesnake. And in an attempt to gain some retribution, Undertaker challenged Austin to a WWE Championship Match at *Fully Loaded*. But this match would be far from traditional. Instead, The Deadman wanted a First Blood Match.

Austin gladly accepted the challenge. For the new champ, it was an opportunity to exact revenge on Undertaker for costing him the WWE Championship against Kane in a First Blood Match at *King of the Ring 1998*. But while Stone Cold had revenge on his mind, Mr. McMahon had even greater aspirations. In the weeks leading up to *Fully Loaded*, McMahon declared that if Austin had lost to Undertaker, he would never again be able to compete for the WWE Championship. On the flip side, however, if The Rattlesnake was able to defeat The Deadman, Mr. McMahon would be gone from WWE forever. Never before had so much been at stake in a single match. It truly was the end of an era for somebody.

The blood war kicked off with both men targeting the other's faces, which were both opened up earlier in the day. But despite their best efforts, neither Undertaker nor Austin were able make the other bleed. Finally, after approximately fifteen minutes of attacks that featured steel steps, ring posts, and the WWE Championship, among other items, Stone Cold nailed Undertaker with a $100,000 television camera. The result of the blow busted The Deadman wide open, giving Austin the win, and marking the end of an era for Mr. McMahon.

OTHER NOTABLE MATCHES

June 28, 1999, *Raw*: Stone Cold Steve Austin defeated Undertaker for the WWE Championship.

May 11, 1997, *In Your House: A Cold Day in Hell*: WWE Champion Undertaker defeated Stone Cold Steve Austin.

August 30, 1998, *SummerSlam*: WWE Champion Stone Cold Steve Austin defeated Undertaker.

May 20, 2001, *Judgment Day*: WWE Champion Stone Cold Steve Austin defeated Undertaker.

MINISTRY OF DARKNESS

Undertaker kicked off a new era of evil in October 1998 when he shockingly reconciled with the abhorrent Paul Bearer. Calling his reunion the Ministry of Darkness, The Deadman promised that he and Bearer would unleash an unholy massacring of the WWE roster, one so great that it would not be comprehensible to those who didn't relish the darkness.

This new Undertaker proved to be the absolute personification of evil. The first Superstar to experience the dark change was Stone Cold Steve Austin, who nearly found himself embalmed alive at the hands of the sadistic Deadman. But believe it or not, embalming another living being was not vicious enough for Undertaker, whose overwhelmingly evil intentions needed an entire army to fully carry out his wishes. So in January 1999, the Lord of Darkness began recruiting members for his demonic Ministry.

Serving as Undertaker's first agents of darkness, The Acolytes abducted a frightened Dennis Knight and handed him over to their new boss. From there, through the power of a chilling ritual, Undertaker transformed Knight into Mideon, the latest member of the Ministry of Darkness. In the weeks that followed, The Brood and Mabel, who Undertaker renamed Viscera, also joined The Deadman's imposing Ministry.

MINISTRY OF DARKNESS

Undertaker	Faarooq	Christian
Paul Bearer	Mideon	Gangrel
Bradshaw	Edge	Viscera

With his Ministry of Darkness in full force, Undertaker continued his unholy attack on WWE, only this time he went straight to the top. In a move guaranteed to get Mr. McMahon's attention, The Deadman kidnapped Stephanie McMahon as *Backlash 1999* went off the air. Mr. McMahon spent the next 24 hours exhausting nearly all his resources in an attempt to find his daughter. But there was no sign of Stephanie or Undertaker.

Stephanie finally resurfaced the next night on *Raw* when the Ministry of Darkness dragged her into the arena kicking and screaming. Undertaker then told Mr. McMahon he would return his daughter safely in exchange for ownership of WWE. Fearing for Stephanie's safety, McMahon agreed to the lofty demand. But when he went to the designated meeting spot to make the swap, nobody was there. Instead, Stephanie was tied to the Undertaker symbol and carried to the ring where she and The Deadman were to join in unholy matrimony.

Both Ken Shamrock and Big Show tried to put an end to the black wedding, but Undertaker's Ministry was too much for them to overcome. Finally, Paul Bearer concluded the disturbing ceremony by telling Undertaker that he may kiss his bride. At that moment, an unlikely hero in the form of Stone Cold Steve Austin came sprinting to the ring to save Stephanie. As a longtime enemy of Mr. McMahon's, Austin was the last person anybody expected to help. But in the end, he chose to put his hatred for Mr. McMahon aside and do the right thing for Stephanie.

"It's me, Austin. It's me, Austin. It was me all along, Austin."

—Mr. McMahon

THE CORPORATE MINISTRY

While Mr. McMahon was preoccupied with his daughter's safety, a power-hungry Shane McMahon swooped in and gained control of The Corporation right out from under his father's nose. With Shane in charge, The Corporation promised to take on a new look, starting with the pilot episode of *SmackDown* in April 1999.

The main event of the show was to feature the pairing of Steve Austin and The Rock battling volunteers from McMahon's Corporation. Triple H quickly raised his hand to be part of the match, but a partner for The Game was still needed. At that moment, Undertaker's music began to play.

"Boys, are you beginning to understand?" asked Shane, who was standing next to Undertaker atop the stage. "Are you beginning to feel the power? Well, let me help spell it out for you just a little bit more."

Then members from both The Corporation and the Ministry of Darkness joined McMahon and Undertaker on stage.

"Austin, Rock... let me be the first to introduce you to the Corporate Ministry," Shane proudly announced. And with that, the merger from Hell was sealed, and two of WWE's most powerful factions combined to become perhaps the most dominant presence WWE had ever seen.

As a member of the Corporate Ministry, Undertaker continued his claim that he was being guided by a mysterious Higher Power. And under this Higher Power, The Deadman continued to target the likes of Stone Cold and The Rock. But as Undertaker's diabolical actions began to intensify, many began to question just who the Higher Power actually was. Many speculated Shane McMahon, others even thought Jake "The Snake" Roberts, but only a select few actually knew the truth. That is until Undertaker chose to reveal the Higher Power on a June 1999 episode of *Raw*. He said:

"For months on end, I prophesized of a power even greater than the Lord of Darkness. I assembled an army to prepare for his eventual arrival. And the Ministry and The Corporation laid the groundwork. So, non-believers, you must prepare for the day of reckoning because it is at hand. So now, as all of us know, it must become apparent to you that he has arrived. So without further ado, I present the Higher Power."

Clad in a dark hooded robe, the mysterious Higher Power slowly made his way down to the ring. The entire sports-entertainment world waited in anxious anticipation. Who was this Higher Power? Who was this devious master of mind games? Who was this man calling the shots for Undertaker? Then came the moment of truth. The Higher Power slowly pulled back his hood to reveal his true self—Mr. McMahon.

TITLE HISTORY

WWE CHAMPIONSHIP

NOVEMBER 27, 1991 – DECEMBER 3, 1991

Only one year after his debut, Undertaker defeated Hulk Hogan for the WWE Championship at *Survivor Series 1991*. While impressive, the victory was not without controversy. The Deadman earned the win after Tombstoning The Hulkster atop a steel object provided by Ric Flair. A short six days later, Undertaker lost the gold back to Hogan at *This Tuesday in Texas*. Much like the original match-up, the rematch was marred by controversy when The Hulkster tossed a handful of ashes from Paul Bearer's urn into Undertaker's face.

MARCH 23, 1997 – AUGUST 3, 1997

Undertaker earned his second WWE Championship at *WrestleMania 13* when he used a Tombstone to effectively end the reign of Sycho Sid. The Deadman went on to carry the gold for more than four months, which proved to be the longest WWE Title reign of his career. After defeating the likes of Stone Cold Steve Austin, Mankind, and Faarooq, Undertaker eventually lost the Title to Bret Hart at *SummerSlam*, largely due to the reckless actions of special guest referee Shawn Michaels.

MAY 19, 2002 – JULY 21, 2002

Barring another Title reign in the future, Undertaker's WWE Championship history will forever be bookended by victories over the legendary Hulk Hogan. More than a decade after defeating The Hulkster for the gold at *Survivor Series 1991*, Big Evil pulled off the feat again when he topped Hogan to capture the Title at *Judgment Day 2002*. A little more than two months later, Undertaker lost the gold without ever being pinned or submitting. The Rock captured the Championship in a Triple Threat Match when he pinned the contest's third participant, Kurt Angle.

MAY 23, 1999 – JUNE 28, 1999

A fast count by special referee Shane McMahon helped Undertaker defeat Stone Cold Steve Austin at *Over the Edge* to claim his third WWE Championship. A little over a month later, Austin exacted his revenge when he regained the gold from The Deadman on *Monday Night Raw*.

88

WORLD HEAVYWEIGHT CHAMPIONSHIP

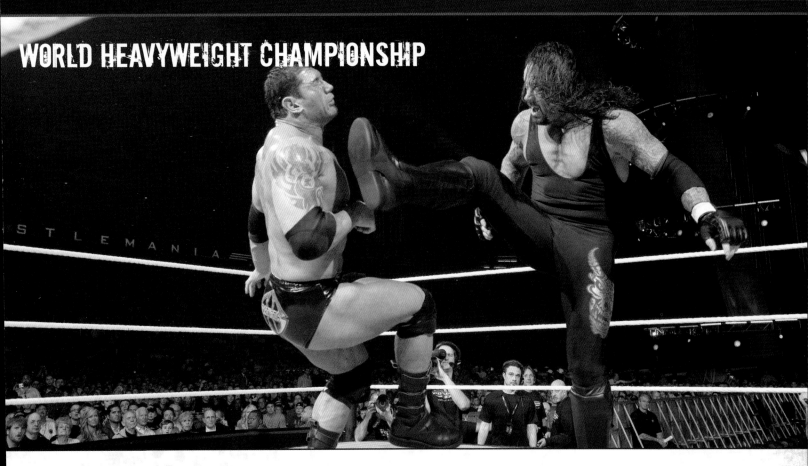

APRIL 1, 2007 – MAY 11, 2007

After winning the 2007 Royal Rumble Match, Undertaker went on to defeat Batista for the World Heavyweight Championship at *WrestleMania 23*. The win made The Deadman the first-ever Superstar to capture both the WWE and World Heavyweight Championships at the Showcase of the Immortals. The following month, Undertaker survived a brutal Steel Cage Match against Batista. But after the contest, Mark Henry viciously attacked The Deadman, making him easy prey for Edge, who cashed in his Money in the Bank briefcase to become World Heavyweight Champion.

MARCH 30, 2008 – MAY 2, 2008

When Undertaker defeated Edge in the main event of *WrestleMania XXIV*, not only did he successfully extend his *WrestleMania* winning streak to 16-0, he also captured his second World Heavyweight Championship. With subsequent victories over the likes of The Rated-R Superstar, as well as Batista, The Phenom appeared to have a firm grasp on the gold. But then came Vickie Guerrero. The then-*SmackDown* General Manager controversially stripped Undertaker of the Title, claiming the chokehold he used was illegal.

OCTOBER 4, 2009 – FEBRUARY 21, 2010

Undertaker's longest World Heavyweight Championship reign kicked off in October 2009 when he beat CM Punk inside Satan's Structure at *Hell in a Cell*. After nearly five months with the title, The Deadman's reign came to a crashing halt at *Elimination Chamber* when Shawn Michaels snuck into the structure and delivered Sweet Chin Music to Undertaker, allowing Chris Jericho to swoop in for the pin and the Championship.

WWE WORLD TAG TEAM CHAMPIONSHIP

JULY 26, 1998 – AUGUST 10, 1998

Undertaker captured his first-ever World Tag Team Championship when he and partner Stone Cold Steve Austin defeated Kane and Mankind in the main event of *Fully Loaded 1998*. The unlikely pairing held the gold for two weeks before Kane and Mankind regained the Titles in a Fatal Four Way Match on *Raw*, which also included the New Age Outlaws, The Rock, and D'Lo Brown.

AUGUST 22, 1999 – AUGUST 30, 1999

Undertaker and Big Show proved to be too much for X-Pac and Kane at *SummerSlam 1999*, as The Unholy Alliance used both a Chokeslam and Tombstone to flatten X-Pac and walk away with the World Tag Team Titles. Eight days later, the Rock 'n' Sock Connection beat Big Show and Undertaker on *Raw* to capture the gold.

SEPTEMBER 9, 1999 – SEPTEMBER 20, 1999

Undertaker and Big Show were not without the World Tag Team Titles for long. Just days after losing to the Rock 'n' Sock Connection, The Unholy Alliance regained the gold in a Buried Alive Match on *SmackDown*, thanks in large part to the interference of Triple H. Much like their first reign, Undertaker and Big Show did not sit atop the tag team mountain long before losing the titles back to The Rock and Mankind in a Dark Side Rules Match on *Raw*.

DECEMBER 18, 2000 – DECEMBER 21, 2000

For three days in December 2000, Undertaker and The Rock were recognized as the best tag team in the business when they defeated Edge and Christian for the World Tag Team Titles on *Raw*. By week's end, however, the gold found its way back around the waists of Edge and Christian when the young duo defeated The Deadman and The Great One on *SmackDown*.

APRIL 19, 2001 – APRIL 29, 2001

When on the same page, Undertaker and Kane are nearly unstoppable, as evidenced by their World Tag Team Championship victory over Edge and Christian on an April 2001 episode of *SmackDown*. The Brothers of Destruction held the gold for ten days before losing it to WWE Champion Stone Cold Steve Austin and Intercontinental Champion Triple H at *Backlash*.

AUGUST 19, 2001 – SEPTEMBER 17, 2001

WCW Tag Team Champions Undertaker and Kane also became WWE World Tag Team Champions when they defeated Diamond Dallas Page and Kanyon for the Titles at *SummerSlam 2001*. It marked the second World Tag Team Championship reign for the Brothers of Destruction, and Undertaker's sixth overall. Nearly a month later, The Dudleys used some help from the interfering Kronik and Stevie Richards to upend Undertaker and Kane for the Titles on *Raw*.

WCW TAG TEAM CHAMPIONSHIP

AUGUST 9, 2001 – SEPTEMBER 27, 2001

While Undertaker remained loyal to WWE during the Monday Night War, he did manage to capture the WCW Tag Team Championship when he and Kane defeated Chuck Palumbo and Sean O'Haire during WCW's 2001 invasion of WWE. The Brothers of Destruction held the Titles for nearly two months before ultimately losing to Booker T and Test on *SmackDown*.

WWE HARDCORE CHAMPION

DECEMBER 9, 2001 – FEBRUARY 7, 2002

When Undertaker defeated Rob Van Dam for the Hardcore Championship at *Vengeance 2001*, he added a stability to the Title that had rarely been seen. In fact, Big Evil's two months with the gold goes down as the fifth longest Hardcore Championship reign of all time. Undertaker eventually lost the Title to Maven on a February 2002 edition of *SmackDown*, thanks in large part to interference by The Rock.

2007 *ROYAL RUMBLE* WINNER

After entering at the No. 30 position, Undertaker eliminated The Great Khali, Montel Vontavious Porter, and finally Shawn Michaels to win the 2007 Royal Rumble Match. With the win, Undertaker became the first Superstar to ever win the Rumble match from the No. 30 position.

AMERICAN BAD ASS

Making rash threats is something Mr. McMahon has done for years. Having those threats ignored, however, is something with which The Chairman has little experience. But that's exactly what happened in September 1999 when Undertaker refused to battle Triple H in a Casket Match, despite McMahon threatening to pull him from the upcoming *Unforgiven* pay-per-view if he didn't. Despite the lofty ultimatum, The Deadman ignored Mr. McMahon and simply walked out of WWE.

More than half a year passed without any sign of The Deadman. Many assumed he was gone for good, while others feared he might reappear in rival WCW. All the speculators, however, were eventually proven dead wrong when Undertaker returned in a major way at *Judgment Day*.

With WWE Champion The Rock and Triple H knotted at five falls apiece and fewer than two minutes to go in *Judgment Day*'s WWE Iron Man Match, odd music began to play over the arena sound system. The strange song did little to stop members of the McMahon-Helmsley Faction from continuing their relentless assault on The Rock. But what happened next certainly did. From out of nowhere, the thunderous sound of a motorcycle began to roar throughout the crowd. Everybody rose to see where the noise was coming from. Finally, after several apprehensive moments, came the shadow of a large man riding through the smoky entranceway. It was Undertaker!

After eight months away, the returning Undertaker was unlike The Deadman the fans once knew. Gone were the macabre characteristics that originally made him so famous, and in their place was a motorcycle-riding American Bad Ass who was looking to take back his yard, starting with the McMahon-Helmsley Faction.

After clearing the ring of Triple H's cohorts, Undertaker focused his attention on The Game. With just seconds left in the match, Undertaker nailed Triple H with a Chokeslam, followed by a Tombstone.

The attack on The Game went a long way in reestablishing Undertaker as a Superstar the fans could trust. Unfortunately, however, it also inadvertently gave a fall to Triple H via disqualification, resulting in The Game winning the WWE Iron Man Match six to five and capturing The Rock's title.

INVASION

Affectionately referred to as the American Bad Ass, the new-look Undertaker wasted no time reminding the locker room that while his appearance may have changed, stepping in the ring with him was just as dangerous as ever. And over the course of the next year, Superstars such as Kurt Angle, The Rock, Chris Jericho, and even Shane McMahon all learned this lesson the hard way.

Undertaker's dominance, however, did little to stop Diamond Dallas Page, who proved crazy enough to target Undertaker in the most personal and intimate way imaginable. While hiding in and around the American Bad Ass's ranch, the invading WCW Superstar voyeuristically stalked Undertaker's wife, recording her most private moments along the way.

Fueled by a master plan that only his mind could justify, DDP showed his recordings to the world. Knowing that stepping into the ring with the great Undertaker would make him famous, Page hoped to enrage the American Bad Ass to the point where an in-ring battle was inevitable. And at *King of the Ring 2001*, DDP got what he wished for—and then some. Fighting for the honor of both his family and company, Undertaker destroyed Page up and down the arena to the point where DDP had no choice but to run away like a coward.

"Page, you're not famous because you suck."

—Undertaker to Diamond Dallas Page

While Undertaker was successful in extinguishing the perverted threats of Diamond Dallas Page, there were still several other invading WCW Superstars hoping to use the American Bad Ass as their launching pad to fame. Among the first in line were Chuck Palumbo and Sean O'Haire, who quickly regretted their decision when they lost their WCW Tag Team Titles to Undertaker and Kane in August 2001. Then, just days later, the Brothers of Destruction historically unified the WCW and WWE Tag Team Titles when they defeated the rival camp's Kanyon and DDP at *SummerSlam*.

By November 2001, the war between WWE and the WCW/ECW Alliance had reached its boiling point. After years of battling back and forth, it was clear that the sports-entertainment landscape at the time only had room for one dominant promotion. So at *Survivor Series*, the two sides squared off in a five-on-five Elimination Match to decide which company would finally be declared the ultimate winner.

Fighting for WWE's survival were Undertaker, Kane, The Rock, Chris Jericho, and Big Show, while The Alliance put their fate in the hands of Rob Van Dam, Booker T, and WWE turncoats Stone Cold Steve Austin, Kurt Angle, and Shane McMahon. In the end, Team WWE was successful in their quest to eradicate The Alliance and forever exterminate WCW from the sports-entertainment world.

BIG EVIL

After more than a year of competing as the motorcycle-riding American Bad Ass, Undertaker had finally won back the fans' trust that he had lost while leading his 1999 Ministry of Darkness. And with Team WWE's victory at *Survivor Series*, Undertaker's popularity amazingly continued to climb to even greater heights. But just as everything seemed to be coming together for the fans and their relationship with the American Bad Ass, Undertaker crushed their hearts yet again.

Just days after helping lead Team WWE to victory at *Survivor Series*, Undertaker did the unimaginable when he forced a defenseless Jim Ross to kiss Mr. McMahon's bare backside. In that one fleeting moment, Undertaker took all the equity he had built up with the fans and threw it away like a meaningless piece of trash. Gone was the American Bad Ass the fans had learned to trust and in his place was Big Evil.

Sporting a more vicious brawling style than ever before, as well as a new tightly cropped hairstyle, the new Undertaker proved to be more ruthless than ever before. And one of the first unfortunate souls to realize this was Rob Van Dam, who lost his Hardcore Championship to Big Evil in a hellacious match at *Vengeance 2001*. Undertaker went on to hold the title for two months, the fifth longest reign in WWE history.

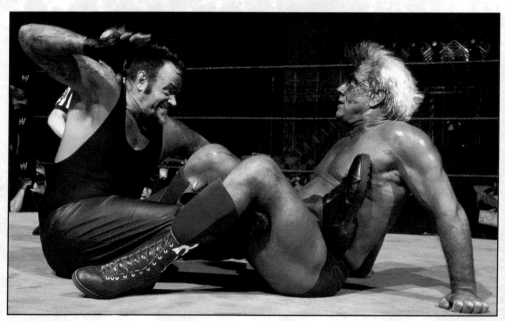

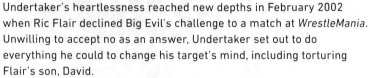

Undertaker's heartlessness reached new depths in February 2002 when Ric Flair declined Big Evil's challenge to a match at *WrestleMania*. Unwilling to accept no as an answer, Undertaker set out to do everything he could to change his target's mind, including torturing Flair's son, David.

While David Flair was training at WWE's facilities in Connecticut, Undertaker showed up unannounced and gave the son of arguably the greatest competitor of all time the beating of a lifetime. Once done, Undertaker sat on the floor, put his arm around his bloody victim, and delivered an earnest message to "The Nature Boy."

"I told you that I wasn't gonna take no for an answer," Undertaker started. "This is your oldest boy here and you know what he means to me? He don't mean a damn thing to me. You know you got what I want, and all it is is a yes. This is on your head, man. 'Cuz I don't give a damn."

As a battered David Flair struggled to get to his feet, Undertaker had one more message for his would-be opponent, a message that was guaranteed to give Big Evil what he wanted—Undertaker threatened to go after the Flair's daughter next. Left with no other choice, "The Nature Boy" finally accepted Undertaker's *WrestleMania* challenge.

With revenge at the forefront of his mind, Flair went right at Undertaker to start the match; he even bloodied Big Evil's cheek early in the contest. But Undertaker quickly returned the favor by busting "The Nature Boy" open with fists of his own.

Toward what appeared to be the end of the match, Undertaker hit a battered Flair with a spine-rattling superplex. The referee quickly dropped to his knees and began to make the count, but before his hand could hit the mat a third time, Undertaker lifted Flair up. The arrogant move revealed to the world the shocking truth that Big Evil was more interested in inflicting pain on "The Nature Boy" than he was in keeping his *WrestleMania* undefeated streak alive.

Undertaker almost lived to regret his hubris when later in the match, Flair's close friend Arn Anderson interfered, nailing Big Evil with a spinebuster. But amazingly, Undertaker was able to quickly recover from The Enforcer's attack and nail Flair with a Tombstone for the victory. The win successfully extended Undertaker's *WrestleMania* undefeated streak to 10-0.

UNDERTAKER VS. HOLLYWOOD HULK HOGAN

Date:	May 19, 2002
Event:	*Judgment Day*
City:	Nashville, Tennessee
Venue:	Gaylord Entertainment Center
Commentators:	Jim Ross, Jerry "The King" Lawler

With his *WrestleMania X8* success behind him, Undertaker shifted his attention toward reclaiming the WWE Championship. And in April 2002, The Phenom took a giant step toward achieving his goal when he defeated Stone Cold Steve Austin in a No. 1 Contender's Match at *Backlash*.

Later that same night, Hulk Hogan completed one of the greatest comebacks in sports-entertainment history when he defeated Triple H for the Undisputed WWE Championship. With the win, *Judgment Day*'s main event was set: Undertaker versus Undisputed WWE Champion Hulk Hogan, the same man Big Evil defeated for his first WWE Championship more than a decade earlier.

For most, simply defeating Hogan for the gold at *Judgment Day* would be enough. But in the weeks leading up to the event, Undertaker revealed that he wanted so much more. Not only did he desire The Hulkster's championship, but he also vowed to be the judge, jury, and executioner of Hulkamania. According to Undertaker, he was going to leave Hogan a bloody shell of a man, while destroying Hulkamania in the process.

Proving he wasn't fazed by Undertaker's threats, Hogan took one of the Red Devil's prized motorcycles and ran it over with an eighteen-wheeler. Unfortunately for The Hulkster, the motorcycle's destruction only accelerated Undertaker's designs to destroy Hulkamania. In the days leading up to *Judgment Day*, Big Evil heartlessly hogtied Hogan to the back of a motorcycle and rode around an arena at high speed with The Hulkster dragging behind. It was clear these two were on a collision course that would eventually explode at *Judgment Day*.

Before the match even started, Undertaker went right at Hogan, attacking the champ with his own yellow weightlifting belt. The Hulkster withstood multiple lashes before finally gaining control of the belt and returning the favor. After several moments, the referee finally snagged the strap and threw it out of play, allowing the match to officially get underway.

As many predicted heading in, the match proved to be an all-out slugfest, both in and out of the ring. Neither Hogan nor Undertaker were concerned with making it a scientific affair; they just wanted to beat each other mercilessly. And that's exactly what they did.

As the match marched on, Undertaker began to focus his attention on Hogan's veteran legs. The strategy was not only a great offensive game plan, but also served as wise defense, as a Leg Drop from a hobbled Hogan, Undertaker assumed, would probably pack less impact. And he was right. Late in the match, Hogan nailed Big Evil with the Big Boot, followed by his signature Leg Drop. But unlike most Hogan Leg Drops, this one failed to end the match. Instead, Undertaker kicked out at two.

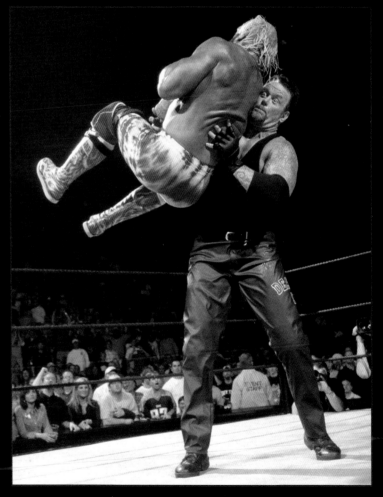

Hogan hit a second Leg Drop, but by this time, Mr. McMahon had rushed the ringside area and occupied much of the referee's attention. An irate Hulkster went right after McMahon, nailing him with a punch and Leg Drop. Unfortunately for Hogan, however, the distraction provided plenty of time for Undertaker to recover and attack The Hulkster from behind. With Hogan weakened, the Red Devil lifted the champ up for a Chokeslam, which marked the end of the match, The Hulkster's sixth championship reign, and his nostalgic ride back at the top.

Conversely, the victory kicked off Undertaker's fourth WWE Championship reign, one that would end in controversy after more than two months.

RIVAL: BROCK LESNAR

SEPTEMBER 22, 2002 - *UNFORGIVEN*

UNDERTAKER VERSUS WWE CHAMPION BROCK LESNAR (DOUBLE DISQUALIFICATION)

Undertaker defended the Undisputed WWE Championship for more than two months before having it taken from him in controversial fashion. While defending the gold against The Rock and Kurt Angle in a Triple Threat Match at *Vengeance*, Undertaker found himself on the outside looking in—The Great One pinned the Olympic gold medalist to win the match, as well as the American Bad Ass's title. It marked the first time in WWE history that a Champion was not involved in the deciding fall of a Triple Threat WWE Championship Match.

Feeling robbed, Undertaker looked to regain what he believed was rightfully his. And when The Rock's reign was cut short by a surging Brock Lesnar at *SummerSlam*, that meant the American Bad Ass had his eyes set on The Next Big Thing, a man with whom he would share an extensive history over the years.

Brock Lesnar's rookie year saw him decimate such legends as Hulk Hogan, Ric Flair, and The Rock, who The Next Big Thing defeated to claim the WWE Championship less than six months into his career. At *Unforgiven*, Lesnar looked to add Undertaker to his list of legends he destroyed when the two squared off with the gold on the line.

To ensure he would have the mental edge heading into the match, Lesnar and his agent, Paul Heyman, kicked off a perverse plan aimed at Undertaker's pregnant wife. The dastardly duo waited until she was alone backstage before approaching and terrifying her. Lesnar slowly backed her against the wall, while she visibly shook in fear. The champ then put his hands on her pregnant stomach and simply said, "Life's a bitch."

The stress from the altercation sent Undertaker's wife into false labor. Luckily, everything ended up being fine with the pregnancy. But the incident transformed the American Bad Ass into an emotional freight train heading into one of the biggest matches of his career.

From the moment the bell rang, it was evident that the match would be both very personal and extremely intense. In fact, it was so hard-hitting that the referee found himself knocked down three separate times throughout the match. On the third and final instance, the official was left with no choice but to declare the match a double disqualification.

OCTOBER 20, 2002 - NO MERCY

WWE CHAMPION BROCK LESNAR DEFEATED UNDERTAKER IN A HELL IN A CELL MATCH

When *Unforgiven* went off the air, fans were left with the image of Undertaker viciously throwing Brock Lesnar through the show's set near the entranceway. While the outcome of the match was disappointing, it gave fans who despised Lesnar a reason to cheer. It also gave Lesnar motivation to seek revenge from the American Bad Ass.

In the days following *Unforgiven*, an upset Lesnar attacked Undertaker from behind on several occasions. One of the attacks, which took place in the backstage area, saw The Next Big Thing nail Undertaker with a propane tank, breaking the legendary veteran's hand in the process.

Despite the broken hand, Undertaker insisted on going through with his rematch against Lesnar at *No Mercy*. To make things even more interesting, the encounter was to be a Hell in a Cell Match.

With four Hell in a Cell Matches to his credit, Undertaker went into the contest with plenty of experience. He also possessed a built-in weapon: his cast. The American Bad Ass used the cast early and often, busting open Lesnar in the early going. Within minutes, it was clear that the combination of Undertaker's experience, his cast, and his emotions would be tough for Lesnar to overcome. But the young champion refused to be intimidated.

Looking to rid Undertaker of his weapon, Lesnar targeted much of his offense on the challenger's hand. He even bit away at the cast, hoping to separate it from Undertaker's body. After several minutes, the champ finally pulled the cast from his opponent's hand, leaving the broken appendage exposed as a prime target.

With Undertaker reeling, Lesnar smashed the challenger with the ring's steel steps, resulting in the American Bad Ass losing blood at an alarming rate. But Undertaker, who was clearly operating on instincts by this time, refused to give up. Amazingly, he found the power to lift Lesnar for a Tombstone, but the champ countered the move into an F5 for the win, marking the end to one of the bloodiest battles in WWE history.

BROCK LESNAR DEFEATED UNDERTAKER

The unthinkable happened at *WrestleMania 30* when Brock Lesnar defeated Undertaker to end The Deadman's *WrestleMania* undefeated streak.

OTHER NOTABLE MATCHES

August 28, 2003, *SmackDown*: Undertaker defeats Brock Lesnar and Big Show in a Triple Threat No. 1 Contender's Match.

October 19, 2003, *No Mercy*: WWE Champion Brock Lesnar defeats Undertaker in a Biker Chain Match.

RETURN OF THE DEADMAN

Undertaker's fifth WWE Championship reign was within reach when he seemingly had Brock Lesnar defeated at *No Mercy* 2003. But before the victory was official, Mr. McMahon interfered on Lesnar's behalf, helping The Next Big Thing successfully fend off Undertaker and retain the title.

Furious over the events of *No Mercy*, Undertaker vowed revenge on Mr. McMahon; luckily for him, he didn't have to wait long to get it. Just days after the pay-per-view, Undertaker won a Triple Threat Match against Lesnar and Big Show. As a result of the victory, the American Bad Ass could name any opponent he wanted for *Survivor Series*. With *No Mercy* fresh in his mind, Undertaker quickly called for the head of Mr. McMahon. But he didn't want to battle the boss in just a traditional contest; instead, Undertaker wanted a Buried Alive Match.

Seemingly scared out of his mind, Mr. McMahon spent the final few moments prior to the match praying to a higher power that he believed would protect him. But there was no protecting the boss on this night. For Undertaker, this was an opportunity to make Mr. McMahon atone for all the years of disrespect, and he wasted no time in making McMahon accountable. Within seconds of the opening bell, Undertaker bloodied the boss and followed up with a beating unlike any seen in recent memory.

Shovels, television monitors, steel ring steps: Undertaker hit McMahon with it all en route to what looked to be the most lopsided victory in the history of Buried Alive Matches. But just when the American Bad Ass tried to open the door to the payloader that carried the dirt, a giant explosion viciously tossed Undertaker backward. Then, from out of nowhere, Kane appeared, throwing his disoriented brother into the grave. Meanwhile, Mr. McMahon covered him with a gigantic mound of dirt for the victory.

On that night, people were forced to question whether Undertaker's amazing thirteen-year career was over. Those who assumed it had, in fact, reached its premature conclusion were further convinced by Undertaker's complete absence over the next few months. But in typical Undertaker fashion, he eventually proved that nothing could keep WWE's most powerful presence down for long.

While competing in the 2004 *Royal Rumble* Match, Kane became distracted when the sound of his brother's signature gong rang out mid-match. The disruption resulted in the Big Red Monster's elimination from the match, but failing to win the *Royal Rumble* would soon be the least of Kane's concerns. Over the ensuing weeks, more omens of Undertaker's imminent return tormented Kane. With each sign, the Big Red Monster became more and more frightened for his wellbeing.

All the torment eventually led to a showdown at *WrestleMania XX*, although Kane wasn't completely convinced his brother would show up—the Big Red Monster still clung to the hope that he ended Undertaker at *Survivor Series*. Unfortunately for Kane, his hope was crushed when Paul Bearer led a band of fire-carrying druids down the Madison Square Garden aisle. And behind them was the one person Kane thought he would never see again: Undertaker, clad in his original Deadman garb.

Kane looked on in complete disbelief as his brother entered the ring. "You are not real," he screamed, as the capacity crowd chanted Undertaker's name. Still not completely convinced, Kane slowly walked up to his brother and gently touched him, just to make sure the figure he saw wasn't a figment of his imagination. At that moment, the Big Red Machine learned the hard way that Undertaker was very real. The Deadman unleashed an all-out assault on the brother that ruthlessly tried to end him at *Survivor Series*.

Like a runaway freight train, Undertaker's offense appeared nearly unstoppable. Conversely, any offense Kane tried to dish out was often rendered useless. In fact, at one point late in the match, Kane hit Undertaker with the signature Chokeslam that had grounded so many greats over the years— but not Undertaker. Instead, The Phenom merely sat up, proving to Kane that he was the superior brother on this night. Shortly after, Undertaker hit a Chokeslam of his own, followed by a Tombstone for the win.

With the victory, Undertaker extended his *WrestleMania* undefeated streak to 12-0. Perhaps more importantly, he also told the sports-entertainment world that The Deadman, the same Creature of the Night that began haunting WWE in 1990, was back for good.

CEMENTING A LEGACY

When Booker T was traded to *SmackDown* in March 2004, the five-time WCW Champion made it clear that he hadn't been paying attention to the pecking order of his new brand. In addition to claiming he was the best Superstar on *SmackDown*, Booker stretched his declaration, exclaiming he was the biggest Superstar in the *history* of *SmackDown*, a history that also included Undertaker.

As expected, The Deadman took exception to the insane claims and confronted Booker T on *SmackDown*. Despite proclaiming earlier in the night that he wasn't afraid of The Phenom, Booker's face showed signs of unvarnished fear once he found himself in the ring with Undertaker. Hoping to extinguish his dread, Booker whacked The Deadman with the urn, but the attack did little to slow Undertaker. At that moment, Booker T wished he had never opened his mouth and began to make his escape. However, he soon learned that his safe haven was only temporary, as it was announced that the arrogant Superstar would battle Undertaker at *Judgment Day* 2004.

Realizing that a victory over Undertaker could solidify his ridiculous claims, Booker T called his *Judgment Day* battle the biggest of his career. He went into it planning to unleash a relentless and focused attack on Undertaker's legs. Though his game plan looked good on paper, it only temporarily slowed The Deadman, who eventually scooped up Booker for the Tombstone and the win, proving to his opponent and everybody watching who the true star of *SmackDown* really was.

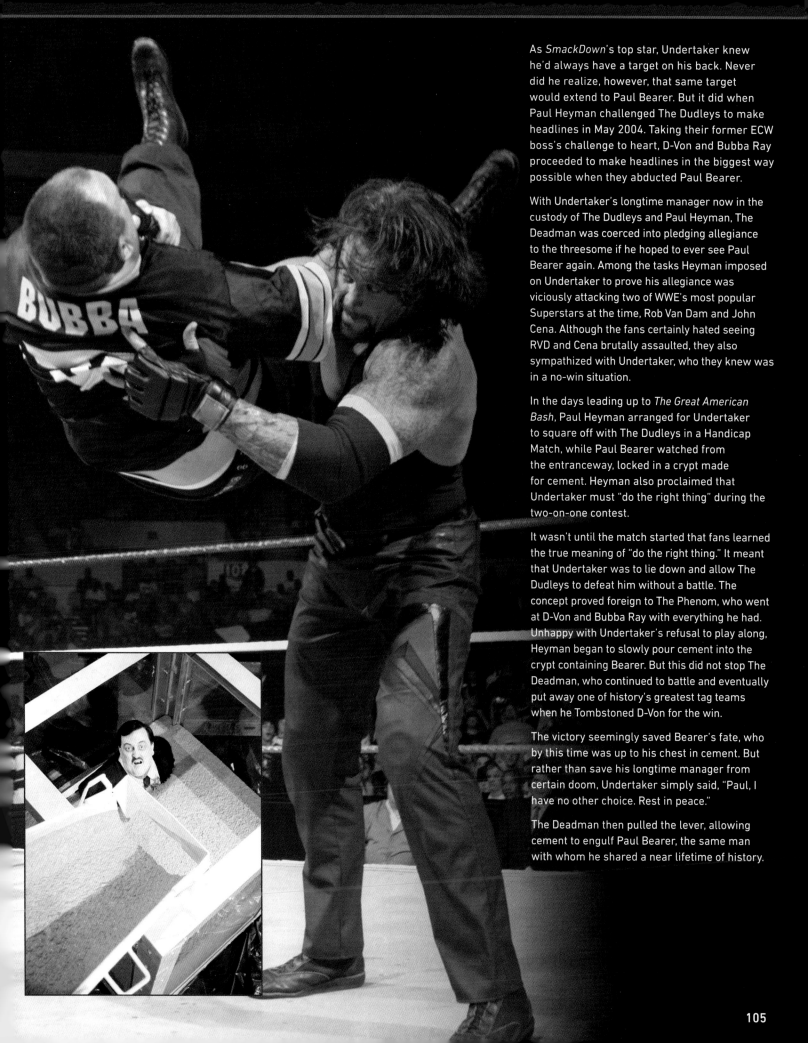

As *SmackDown*'s top star, Undertaker knew he'd always have a target on his back. Never did he realize, however, that same target would extend to Paul Bearer. But it did when Paul Heyman challenged The Dudleys to make headlines in May 2004. Taking their former ECW boss's challenge to heart, D-Von and Bubba Ray proceeded to make headlines in the biggest way possible when they abducted Paul Bearer.

With Undertaker's longtime manager now in the custody of The Dudleys and Paul Heyman, The Deadman was coerced into pledging allegiance to the threesome if he hoped to ever see Paul Bearer again. Among the tasks Heyman imposed on Undertaker to prove his allegiance was viciously attacking two of WWE's most popular Superstars at the time, Rob Van Dam and John Cena. Although the fans certainly hated seeing RVD and Cena brutally assaulted, they also sympathized with Undertaker, who they knew was in a no-win situation.

In the days leading up to *The Great American Bash*, Paul Heyman arranged for Undertaker to square off with The Dudleys in a Handicap Match, while Paul Bearer watched from the entranceway, locked in a crypt made for cement. Heyman also proclaimed that Undertaker must "do the right thing" during the two-on-one contest.

It wasn't until the match started that fans learned the true meaning of "do the right thing." It meant that Undertaker was to lie down and allow The Dudleys to defeat him without a battle. The concept proved foreign to The Phenom, who went at D-Von and Bubba Ray with everything he had. Unhappy with Undertaker's refusal to play along, Heyman began to slowly pour cement into the crypt containing Bearer. But this did not stop The Deadman, who continued to battle and eventually put away one of history's greatest tag teams when he Tombstoned D-Von for the win.

The victory seemingly saved Bearer's fate, who by this time was up to his chest in cement. But rather than save his longtime manager from certain doom, Undertaker simply said, "Paul, I have no other choice. Rest in peace."

The Deadman then pulled the lever, allowing cement to engulf Paul Bearer, the same man with whom he shared a near lifetime of history.

RIVAL: RANDY ORTON

UNDERTAKER DEFEATED RANDY ORTON

By 2005, Randy Orton had solidified himself as one of the biggest stars in all of sports-entertainment. Not only was Orton a third-generation Superstar, but he was also the youngest World Heavyweight Champion in WWE history, and a man whose resume already included the slayings of legends Mick Foley, Ric Flair, Sgt. Slaughter, and Jake "The Snake" Roberts.

Orton's callous attacks on the great names that helped build the sports-entertainment industry earned him the "Legend Killer" moniker. And at *WrestleMania 21*, Orton looked to end one of the biggest legends of them all: Undertaker.

It was The Legend versus The Legend Killer. Despite the grand stage of *WrestleMania*, the young, brash, and arrogant Randy Orton claimed he had no fear of Undertaker, which he proved by slapping The Deadman across the face to start the match.

The impudent move did nothing more than set The Phenom off on a focused offensive assault featuring vintage Undertaker maneuvers such as Old School and a legdrop on the ring apron.

Later in the match, Undertaker shoved his way out of an RKO. The force of the push sent Orton flying into the referee, who was subsequently knocked out of commission for several moments. With the official down, Orton's Hall of Fame-father, Bob Orton, came to the ring and whacked Undertaker with his signature cast. The ref awoke to find The Legend Killer atop a seemingly unconscious Deadman.

The referee began the count, "1 ... 2 ...," and just before the third-and-final count could be made, Undertaker got his shoulder off the mat. He wasn't out of the woods yet. An RKO soon followed, but the result was the same; Undertaker refused to stay down. A frustrated Orton then turned to The Phenom's own signature move, the Tombstone, in an attempt to put him away. But once Orton got Undertaker up, The Deadman reversed the move and delivered a match-ending Tombstone to Orton, thus proving The Legend was superior to The Legend Killer.

AUGUST 21, 2005 - *SUMMERSLAM*
RANDY ORTON DEFEATED UNDERTAKER

After falling to Undertaker at *WrestleMania*, Randy Orton knew his *SummerSlam* encounter with The Deadman was a must-win if he wanted to validate his Legend Killer moniker. To ensure victory would be his, Orton concocted an underhanded plan that would play out in the latter portions of the match.

Hoping to take away Undertaker's vertical game, Orton spent much of the match focusing his offense on The Phenom's legs. The plan worked, as Undertaker could barely put any weight on his left leg. But despite the attack, a hobbled Undertaker battled back and delivered a series of signature Deadman moves, including Old School and a Chokeslam. But just when it appeared Undertaker had the match won, a fan rushed the ring, causing great confusion. The distraction gave Orton the perfect opportunity to sneak behind The Deadman and deliver a devastating RKO to end the match.

When the contest was over, it was revealed that the fan was The Legend Killer's dad, Cowboy Bob Orton. The revelation infuriated Undertaker, who darted toward the fleeing Ortons. With The Deadman in hot pursuit, it was clear that this rivalry was far from over.

DECEMBER 18, 2005 - *ARMAGEDDON*
UNDERTAKER DEFEATED RANDY ORTON IN A HELL IN A CELL MATCH

In the months leading up to *Armageddon*, Randy Orton took his Legend Killer moniker a bit too literally when he launched a series of attacks on Undertaker that would've ended a mortal man. First, Orton and his father locked The Deadman inside a casket at *No Mercy* and proceeded to set it on fire. The following month, Orton tossed a battered Undertaker into a car and backed it into the *SmackDown* stage at a high rate of speed, causing a gigantic explosion. Luckily Undertaker walked away from both attacks, and he sought revenge at *Armageddon* when he battled Orton inside Hell in a Cell.

As expected, the match was both brutal and bloody, with both Superstars using whatever weapons they could get their hands on, including steel chains and the Cell itself. Late in the match, Undertaker accidentally floored the referee with an errant fist. A second referee immediately opened the Cell's door to check on his colleague. This allowed Bob Orton to sneak in and go after The Phenom, which many assumed indicated the end of Undertaker. But in actuality, the Cowboy ended up paying for his sins when he was the recipient of a Tombstone. Shortly thereafter, Undertaker scooped up The Legend Killer and delivered yet another Tombstone. This one, however, was followed by a three count. The Undertaker had finally dismissed Orton. And after the match, The Deadman celebrated his victory atop the Cell with his signature urn in hand.

OTHER NOTABLE MATCHES:

- **May 30, 2002, *SmackDown*:** WWE Undisputed Champion Undertaker defeats Randy Orton.
- **October 9, 2005, *No Mercy*:** Randy and Bob Orton defeat Undertaker in a Handicap Casket Match.
- **February 9, 2009, *Raw*:** Undertaker defeats Randy Orton via disqualification.

THE STREAK

When it comes to succeeding on the grandest stage of them all, there is nobody better than Undertaker. The owner of sports-entertainment's most storied undefeated streak, The Deadman walked out of more than 20 *WrestleMania* matches without suffering a single loss. Shawn Michaels, Ric Flair, Triple H, Kane, Edge...so many all-time greats tried to be the one to end the prodigious streak, but for twenty-one straight matches, none of them were ever able to stop the legendary Undertaker.

WRESTLEMANIA VII

OPPONENT: JIMMY "SUPERFLY" SNUKA

STREAK
1-0

In front of a sold-out Los Angeles Memorial Sports Arena, Undertaker kicked off his illustrious *WrestleMania* undefeated streak when he made short work of Jimmy Snuka, defeating the "Superfly" with a Tombstone after a little more than four minutes of action.

OPPONENT: JAKE "THE SNAKE" ROBERTS

After surviving a series of DDTs, Undertaker nailed Jake Roberts with a Tombstone on the outside before rolling "The Snake" in for the pin and his second straight *WrestleMania* win.

WRESTLEMANIA IX
OPPONENT: GIANT GONZALES

Undertaker's third consecutive *WrestleMania* victory came via disqualification when Giant Gonzales was disqualified for attempting to literally end The Deadman with the use of chloroform.

WRESTLEMANIA XI

OPPONENT: KING KONG BUNDY

Not even the immense girth of King Kong Bundy could prevent Undertaker from bodyslamming and clotheslining the big man, en route to his fourth straight *WrestleMania* victory.

WRESTLEMANIA XII

OPPONENT: DIESEL

Undertaker proved to be the better big man at *WrestleMania XII* when he defeated Diesel following a Tombstone.

WRESTLEMANIA 13

OPPONENT: SYCHO SID

Undertaker's first-ever *WrestleMania* main event was not only the site of The Deadman's second WWE Championship victory, but it also extended his undefeated streak to six when he defeated Sycho Sid.

WRESTLEMANIA XIV

OPPONENT: KANE

In a battle of brothers, it took three Tombstones for Undertaker to turn back Kane and his reprehensible manager, Paul Bearer, at *WrestleMania XIV*.

WRESTLEMANIA XV
OPPONENT: BIG BOSS MAN

Inside the unfriendly confines of Hell in a Cell, Undertaker Tombstoned Big Boss Man to earn his eighth straight *WrestleMania* victory.

WRESTLEMANIA X-SEVEN

OPPONENT: TRIPLE H

In his first of three *WrestleMania* matches against Triple H, Undertaker took the battle out into the Reliant Astrodome crowd, on the way to his ninth straight victory.

STREAK
9-0

WRESTLEMANIA X8
OPPONENT: RIC FLAIR

Undertaker survived an attack from an interfering Arn Anderson to put Ric Flair away and extend his undefeated streak to ten at *WrestleMania X8*.

WRESTLEMANIA XIX

OPPONENT: BIG SHOW AND A-TRAIN

Not even being outnumbered two-to-one could derail Undertaker in his *WrestleMania XIX* battle against A-Train and Big Show.

WRESTLEMANIA XX

OPPONENT: KANE

The Deadman returned at *WrestleMania XX* to once again put away his brother, Kane, and extend his streak to twelve.

WRESTLEMANIA 21

OPPONENT: RANDY ORTON

Not even The Legend Killer himself could end Undertaker's streak. Instead, like so many before him, Randy Orton fell victim to The Phenom's Tombstone at *WrestleMania 21*.

WRESTLEMANIA 22
OPPONENT: MARK HENRY

Not only did Mark Henry learn that you don't test Undertaker at *WrestleMania*, he also found out that you definitely don't do it in a Casket Match.

WRESTLEMANIA 23
OPPONENT: BATISTA

STREAK
15-0

In defeating Batista at *WrestleMania 23*, Undertaker successfully extended his undefeated streak to fifteen, while also capturing the World Heavyweight Championship.

WRESTLEMANIA XXIV

OPPONENT: EDGE

For the second year in a row, Undertaker captured the World Heavyweight Championship at *WrestleMania*, this time by defeating Edge via submission. The win marked Undertaker's first-ever submission victory at *WrestleMania*.

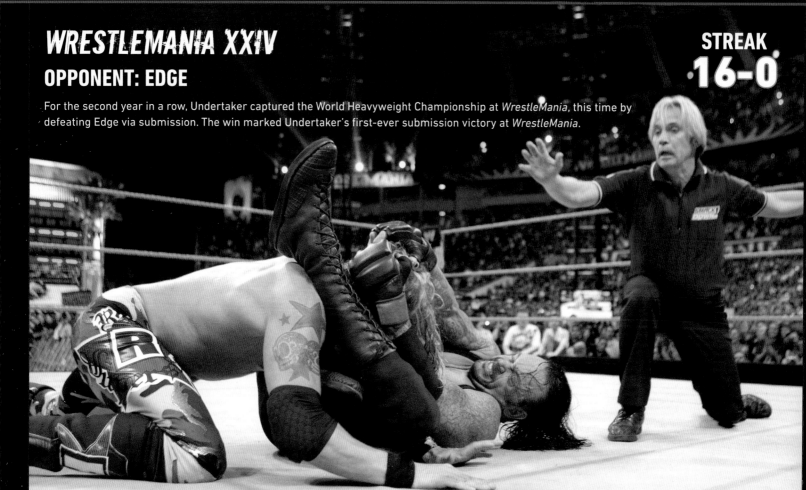

WRESTLEMANIA XXV

STREAK
17-0

OPPONENT: SHAWN MICHAELS

In one of the greatest matches ever contested, Undertaker used the power of his patented Tombstone to turn back Shawn Michaels and become 17-0 at *WrestleMania*.

WRESTLEMANIA XXVI

STREAK 18-0

OPPONENT: SHAWN MICHAELS

Undertaker ended the legendary career of Shawn Michaels at
WrestleMania XXVI when he defeated him in a thrilling
Streak vs. Career Match.

WRESTLEMANIA XXVII
OPPONENT: TRIPLE H

Looking to do what Shawn Michaels couldn't do the prior two years, Triple H squared off against Undertaker at *WrestleMania XXVII*. But much like his close friend, The Game couldn't overcome the powerful force of The Phenom.

WRESTLEMANIA XXVIII

OPPONENT: TRIPLE H

Seeking another chance at immortality, Triple H battled Undertaker inside Hell in a Cell at *WrestleMania XXVIII*. But despite longtime friend Shawn Michaels serving as special guest referee, Triple H was unable to defeat The Deadman.

WRESTLEMANIA 29

OPPONENT: CM PUNK

In his final victory of The Streak, Undertaker turned back CM Punk to go 21-0 and defend the honor of longtime friend Paul Bearer.

WORLD HEAVYWEIGHT CHAMPION

When Undertaker tossed Shawn Michaels over the top rope at the 2007 *Royal Rumble*, he did something he'd never done before in his illustrious career: he won the *Royal Rumble* Match. As a result of the victory, The Deadman had his choice of which titlist to face at *WrestleMania*. In the end, he chose Batista with the hope that he could once again fill out his resume with something that had so far eluded him, the World Heavyweight Championship.

Prior to The Animal and The Deadman squaring off under the bright lights of *WrestleMania*, Mr. McMahon announced that the soon-to-be opponents would actually be partners at *No Way Out* when they squared off against the team of John Cena and HBK. Tensions between Batista and Undertaker were already fevered heading into the event, and by the match's end they undoubtedly reached their boiling point when The Animal turned on The Phenom, delivering a bone-crunching spinebuster in the process.

By *WrestleMania*, each Superstar was anxious to get at the other, as Batista proved by spearing Undertaker within seconds of the match's opening bell. The Animal's lightning quick strike was a sign of what was to come in this World Heavyweight Championship match. It was also proof that Batista was not intimidated by Undertaker, something The Animal stressed heavily in the weeks leading up to the event.

As the match marched on, Batista also proved he would not be overpowered by Undertaker. At one point, The Deadman flattened The Animal with what appeared to be a match-ending Last Ride, but Batista refused to stay down, kicking out at the two count. Moments later, the same thing happened again, when The Animal miraculously survived a Chokeslam.

Showing his own survival skills, Undertaker successfully withstood a heavy offensive spurt by Batista, which featured a spear and Batista Bomb. After kicking out, The Deadman refused to be denied, as he lifted Batista for the Tombstone and drove him straight down into the mat for the win.

With the victory, Undertaker not only extended his *WrestleMania* undefeated streak to 15-0, he also captured the coveted World Heavyweight Championship for the first time in his legendary career.

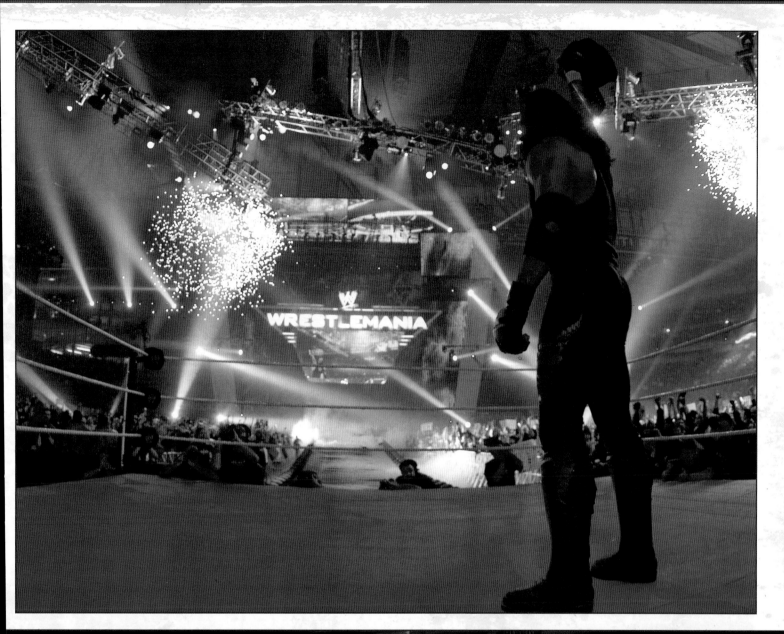

"God help us now. The Undertaker as World Champion. The Lord of Darkness is reigning again."

—Commentator JBL

THE ULTIMATE OPPORTUNIST KNOCKS

Looking to regain the gold, Batista challenged Undertaker in a Last Man Standing Match later that same month at *Backlash*. But when the match's conclusion proved inconclusive due to neither competitor being able to answer the referee's ten-count, another rematch was scheduled. This time, The Animal and The Phenom clashed inside a steel cage.

Unbelievably, the conclusion of the second rematch ended up being just as inconclusive as the first, as both Superstars escaped the cage at the same exact time. The referee had no choice but to declare the match a draw, meaning Undertaker and Batista appeared to be on their way to yet another rematch. Mark Henry and Edge, however, had other plans.

After the grueling Steel Cage Match, Undertaker was inexplicably attacked from behind by Henry. The brutal assault went on for several minutes and by the time it had ended, The Deadman was left motionless in the middle of the ring.

Realizing Undertaker was a sitting duck, Edge quickly grabbed his Money in the Bank briefcase and hit the ring. Once there, he covered Undertaker for what seemed to be an easy win, but The Phenom kicked out at two. Edge covered Undertaker again; but the results were the same. Finally, Edge stood up and waited for The Deadman to reach his feet. When he did, the Rated-R Superstar delivered a rib-rattling spear and went for the cover. This time, there was no getting up for Undertaker. Edge had captured his first World Heavyweight Championship.

Following his victory over Undertaker, Edge spent months successfully escaping the wrath of The Deadman. But when Undertaker won a No. 1 Contender's Elimination Chamber Match at *No Way Out 2008*, the Rated-R Superstar was left with nowhere to run. The main event of *WrestleMania XXIV* was set in stone: Undertaker vs. Edge for the World Heavyweight Championship.

In the year leading up to *WrestleMania*, Edge solidified himself as WWE's Ultimate Opportunist. And as his match with Undertaker drew near, a confident Edge saw his title defense against The Deadman as the opportunity he needed to cement his legacy.

Having never lost to Undertaker, Edge walked to the ring with extreme confidence. But despite his past success against The Phenom, the Rated-R Superstar's initial game plan was flawed. When the opening bell rang, Edge went right for Undertaker with a series of fists. As he soon learned, though, getting into a slugfest with The Deadman was a bad idea.

Edge's gaffe led to Undertaker gaining the early advantage, which steamrolled well into the heart of the match. Unbelievably, however, The Deadman had great difficulty in delivering the final blow, despite going at Edge with all his signature moves. Chokeslam, Old School, Last Ride, Tombstone...Somehow Edge countered them all.

Late in the match, Undertaker inadvertently knocked the referee out with a Big Boot, allowing The Ultimate Opportunist to take liberties he wouldn't normally get away with, including commandeering a television camera with which to whack The Deadman. But that did little to slow Undertaker. Instead, The Phenom simply sat up, scooped up Edge and delivered a Tombstone. The referee, however, was still out cold.

A second referee sprinted toward the ring, but was too late. Edge had recovered before his shoulders could be counted down for three. Following the Tombstone, Edge's allies Curt Hawkins and Zack Ryder hit the ring. While they were unsuccessful in administering any offense on Undertaker, they did distract him long enough for Edge to land a spear on The Phenom.

Shockingly, the spear failed to put Undertaker away, so Edge went for yet another. Only this time, after hitting The Deadman with his signature move, Edge somehow found himself locked in Undertaker's Hell's Gate submission. Unable to reach the ropes, Edge was left with no other option but to tap out, giving Undertaker the win, the World Heavyweight Championship, and his sixteenth straight *WrestleMania* victory.

OVERCOMING CONTROVERSY

Unfortunately for Undertaker, his second World Heavyweight Championship reign was marred with controversy. After The Phenom forced Edge to tap out to Hell's Gate yet again at *Backlash*, the Rated-R Superstar's fiancée and *SmackDown* General Manager Vickie Guerrero stripped The Deadman of the title, claiming his submission move was an illegal chokehold.

More than a year passed before Undertaker was declared World Heavyweight Champion again. At *Breaking Point 2009*, The Deadman forced champion CM Punk to submit to the Hell's Gate, seemingly awarding Undertaker the title in the process. But new General Manager Theodore Long emerged from the back to announce that he had no designs on lifting Vickie Guerrero's ban of Hell's Gate. As a result of Long's decision, the match continued and it wasn't long before Undertaker found himself locked in Punk's Anaconda Vise. Oddly, within seconds of the hold being applied, the referee called for the bell and awarded the match to Punk, despite Undertaker never submitting.

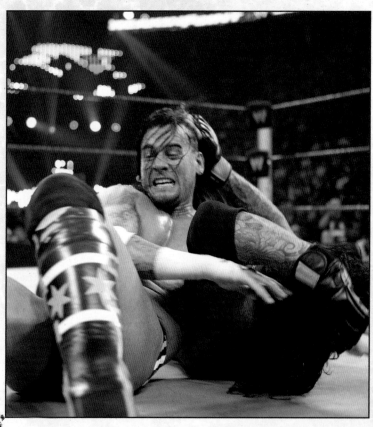

AN UNFORTUNATE COINCIDENCE

Undertaker getting screwed out of the World Heavyweight Championship at *Breaking Point* took place in the same arena that Bret Hart was screwed out of the WWE Championship in 1997, the Bell Centre (formerly the Molson Centre).

Theodore Long later admitted that the controversial conclusion of *Breaking Point* was a pre-mediated plan devised to keep Undertaker from winning the title. After making the bold admission, a worried Long asked for Undertaker's forgiveness. The Deadman, however, had no compassion for the man that screwed him out of the gold. Instead, Undertaker abducted Long in a smoke-filled limo and drove away.

Elsewhere, an unconcerned CM Punk was bragging about beating The Phenom at *Breaking Point* when an ominous band of druids carried a casket to the ring. Assuming it carried Undertaker, Punk cautiously approached the casket ready to defend himself. But when he opened it, he didn't find The Deadman. Instead, a visibly shaken Theodore Long emerged with bad news for Punk:

"You will defend the World Heavyweight Championship against Undertaker inside Hell in a Cell," said a traumatized Long. Realizing his championship reign was in serious jeopardy, Punk simply dropped to his knees and began to assess the torture he was about to endure.

As Punk feared, Satan's Structure proved to be torturous right from the start, as Undertaker almost immediately began using the steel of the Cell as a weapon. With no remorse, The Deadman's game plan never wavered. He simply rammed the Second City Saint's body into the unforgiving steel as often as possible.

Hoping to stop Undertaker's relentless attack, Punk began targeting The Phenom's knees. The move proved wise, as it eventually gave Punk an opening on which he could capitalize. Hobbling, Undertaker climbed the ropes in an attempt to hit Punk with Old School. While at the top, however, The Deadman's knee appeared to buckle, while Punk simultaneously jerked Undertaker off the rope and nailed him with a kick. The Straight Edge Superstar appeared to have The Deadman right where he wanted him.

But on this night, after continually being robbed of the World Heavyweight Championship, Undertaker refused to be denied. Shortly after failing Old School, The Phenom fired back by delivering a signature Chokeslam to the champ followed by a Tombstone. The vicious combination was enough to put Punk away and award Undertaker his third World Heavyweight Championship.

Over the next four-plus months, Undertaker successfully turned back all comers, including Big Show, Batista, and Rey Mysterio. And in February 2010, it appeared The Deadman was about to survive a grueling title defense inside the Elimination Chamber. But in the closing moments of the match, Shawn Michaels snuck into the chamber and delivered Sweet Chin Music to Undertaker, allowing Chris Jericho to make the cover and capture the World Heavyweight Championship.

UNDERTAKER VS. SHAWN MICHAELS

Date:	March 28, 2010
Event:	*WrestleMania XXVI*
City:	Glendale, Arizona
Venue:	University of Phoenix Stadium
Commentators:	Michael Cole, Jerry "The King" Lawler, Matt Striker

For decades, sports-entertainment fans routinely recognized the 1987 battle between Randy Savage and Ricky Steamboat as the greatest match in *WrestleMania* history. Then came 2009 and the epic encounter between Undertaker and Shawn Michaels at *WrestleMania 25*. After more than thirty minutes of heart-pounding suspense, the clash between HBK and The Deadman moved to the top of many historians' lists of greatest matches of all time, and rightfully so.

In the end, Undertaker stood victorious after a Michaels's moonsault landed HBK right in the arms of a waiting Deadman. One Tombstone later and Undertaker extended his *WrestleMania* undefeated streak to 17-0.

Michaels spent the next year agonizing over the loss. According to HBK, if it hadn't been for that one moonsault, he would've been the one to end Undertaker's legendary streak. But it just wasn't meant to be, and HBK became yet another statistic in sports-entertainment's greatest spectacle, The Streak.

As *WrestleMania XXVI* neared, HBK became obsessed with climbing back into the ring with The Deadman. But his dreams were ultimately dashed when Undertaker refused Michaels's request for a *WrestleMania* rematch. This left HBK with no other choice but to force The Phenom to agree. And to do this, Michaels knew he had to take away the one thing he coveted most, the World Heavyweight Championship.

With only Chris Jericho standing in his way, Undertaker looked well on his way to successfully defending his title inside a grueling Elimination Chamber match in February 2010. But just when it looked like The Deadman had things in hand, HBK snuck into the Chamber and delivered Sweet Chin Music to Undertaker, costing him the World Heavyweight Championship in the process.

As Michaels predicted, being the man responsible for Undertaker losing the title forced The Phenom to change his tune when it came to a *WrestleMania* rematch. With revenge at the forefront of his mind, The Deadman finally accepted HBK's challenge, but on one condition: if Michaels lost, his career would be over. Blinded by his desire to make up for his *WrestleMania 25* defeat, HBK agreed to the stipulation, despite its lofty consequences.

In front of more than seventy-two-thousand screaming fans, the two legends stared at each other in the middle of the ring, waiting for the opening bell. One had sports-entertainment's greatest streak on the line, while the other was fighting for his more than twenty-five year-career. When the bell finally rang, it was clear that this match would be just as thrilling as their encounter one year earlier.

In a similar scene to *WrestleMania 25*, both Undertaker and HBK found ways to either counter the other's signature moves or kick out of them. Chokeslam. Tombstone. Last Ride. Hell's Gate. HBK countered or kicked out of each of them. Conversely, Undertaker did the same when Michaels hit him with Sweet Chin Music on several occasions. At one point, Sweet Chin Music even sent The Phenom atop the ringside announce table. From there, Michaels landed a gravity-defying moonsault from the top rope. It appeared as though the only thing standing between HBK and victory was getting The Deadman back in the ring.

Finally back on the inside, HBK went for Sweet Chin Music yet again. But Undertaker countered it into a Chokeslam, followed by a Tombstone. The combination would've put away a lesser man. But Michaels managed to kick out at two.

A look of disbelief fell over Undertaker's face. "Stay down," he screamed to HBK, almost as if to say he didn't want to have to hurt Michaels any further. But The Deadman's moment of compassion fell on deaf ears, as HBK struggled to his feet and slapped Undertaker across the face.

Michaels's slap infuriated The Phenom, who quickly scooped HBK up and delivered a leaping Tombstone for the win in one of the most thrilling matches of all time. The Arizona crowd erupted in celebration of Undertaker's eighteenth straight *WrestleMania* win. But then a somberness quickly rushed over them as they began to realize one of history's greatest careers had just come to an abrupt end.

Respectfully, Undertaker helped Michaels to his feet, shook his hand, and hugged him before disappearing, allowing HBK to soak in the incredible adulation he was receiving from the WWE Universe.

RIVAL: SHAWN MICHAELS

Throughout much of its historic battle with WCW, WWE could always rely on two Superstars: Undertaker and Shawn Michaels. While others such as Kevin Nash, Scott Hall, and Hulk Hogan jumped ship, the loyalty of The Deadman and HBK never wavered. And as cornerstones of the WWE, Undertaker and Michaels found themselves on opposite sides of the ring on several memorable occasions.

JANUARY 18, 1998 - *ROYAL RUMBLE*
WWE CHAMPION SHAWN MICHAELS DEFEATED UNDERTAKER IN A CASKET MATCH

With his eyes set squarely on regaining the gold, Undertaker battled WWE Champion Shawn Michaels in a Casket Match at the *Royal Rumble*. And given The Deadman's legendary history in such matches, Michaels had every right to be afraid. But he wasn't. Instead, HBK knew there was strength in numbers. With D-Generation X by his side, he certainly had the numbers.

Much of the early match belonged to Undertaker, who focused his attack on HBK's back. At one point, The Deadman even backdropped Michaels out of the ring onto the ringside casket, further damaging Michaels's already injured back.

But HBK fired back and eventually nailed Sweet Chin Music before rolling Undertaker into the casket. Before closing the lid, Michaels arrogantly stood over his fallen foe and delivered his patented crotch chop. HBK's showmanship proved ill-timed, as The Deadman simultaneously grabbed Michaels by the crotch and tossed him back into the ring.

Back on the offensive, Undertaker hit HBK with a Chokeslam and Tombstone into the casket. It appeared as though Michaels's reign atop WWE was over. But before The Phenom could close the casket, he was attacked by the New Age Outlaws and Los Boricuas.

The six-on-one attack appeared to seal Undertaker's fate. But just when all hope seemed lost, Kane came to the ring to apparently help his older brother. In reality, though, his sole motive was to end The Deadman himself. After clearing the ring of Undertaker's attackers, the Big Red Monster Chokeslammed his brother into the casket and closed the lid. Then, in one of the most disgusting scenes in WWE history, Kane torched the casket with Undertaker locked inside.

APRIL 5, 2009 - *WRESTLEMANIA 25*
UNDERTAKER DEFEATED SHAWN MICHAELS

Blessed with an amazing career and personal life, a joyous Shawn Michaels took to WWE television to tell the entire world that he believed he was living heaven on the earth. The only thing that could make his life better, he claimed, would be facing Undertaker at *WrestleMania*. Never one to back down, The Deadman accepted HBK's challenge, but reminded him that sometimes it's hell to get to heaven.

Their entrances told a story of darkness versus light, as Undertaker emerged via his traditional ominous entrance, while Michaels, clad in all white, descended from high in the air with countless bright lights leading his way to the ring.

HBK used his quickness to gain an early advantage, but it wasn't long before Undertaker's power game kicked in. For several minutes, both Superstars played to their strengths, as the capacity crowd in Houston struggled to pick a favorite.

Later in the match, Undertaker dodged Sweet Chin Music then countered a figure four into the dreaded Hell's Gate. But Michaels was able to get to the ropes to break the hold. The series of moves was just the first in a long and breathtaking series of counters and kickouts of each Superstar's signature moves.

Finally, after nailing Undertaker with everything he had, including several renditions of Sweet Chin Music, HBK took to the air in an attempt to end it once and for all. But Michaels's moonsault actually placed him perfectly into the arms of Undertaker, who Tombstoned HBK for the win.

With the victory, The Deadman extended his *WrestleMania* undefeated streak to 17-0 and he, alongside HBK, forever etched his name in the history books as a competitor in arguably the greatest match ever contested.

OTHER NOTABLE MATCHES:

- **September 7, 1997, *In Your House: Ground Zero*:** Undertaker vs. Shawn Michaels ended in a no-contest.

- **October 5, 1997, *In Your House: Badd Blood*:** Shawn Michaels defeated Undertaker in a Hell in a Cell match.

- **March 28, 2010, *WrestleMania XXVI*:** Undertaker defeated Shawn Michaels.

BROTHERLY HATRED

Eyeing another World Heavyweight Championship reign, Undertaker qualified to be one of the four Superstars competing for Jack Swagger's gold at *Fatal 4-Way 2010*. But in the days leading up the event, the WWE Universe learned that tragedy had befallen The Phenom.

"Ladies and gentlemen," began *SmackDown* General Manager Theodore Long, "it is with great regret that I must inform you that the Undertaker was found by his brother, Kane, in a vegetative state."

Anguishing over the perceived loss of his brother, Kane vowed to personally persecute anybody responsible for the tragedy. Claiming they would soon be committed to a torturous existence, the Big Red Monster set out on an exhaustive hunt that saw him question a number of Superstars, most notably CM Punk, Rey Mysterio, Jack Swagger, and Big Show.

By *SummerSlam*, not only had Kane defeated Mysterio for the World Heavyweight Championship, but the Big Red Monster also tapped The Ultimate Underdog as Undertaker's sole assailant.

"For sixty days and sixty nights, I have sat at my brother's bedside, waiting as he suffered silently," said Kane. "Then the unthinkable happened. My brother moved and he could manage to utter only two words. Those two words were the name of his assailant. The man who attacked my brother is Rey Mysterio."

With Undertaker's attacker supposedly pinpointed, Kane vowed revenge was near. But simply defeating Mysterio wasn't going to be enough for the Big Red Monster. He wanted more. He wanted to end Mysterio by shoving him into a casket at *SummerSlam*, which Kane nearly accomplished. After defeating Mysterio

with a Chokeslam, the Big Red Monster opened the ringside casket in an attempt to lay his opponent to rest. But instead of finding an empty casket, Kane saw something he never imagined he'd see again, his brother, Undertaker.

Kane backpedaled in disbelief. But there was no getting away from The Phenom. After setting Mysterio free, Undertaker turned to his brother and attacked, revealing that Kane was the true assailant all along.

A BROKEN BROTHERHOOD

"What was once your holy grail is now my World Heavyweight Championship," the conniving Kane told Undertaker, as he beamed with pride over betraying the bond of brotherhood he once shared with The Deadman.

Undertaker responded by telling Kane that he was not worthy of being champion, and even less worthy of being his brother. And at *Night of Champions*, The Deadman planned to exact revenge by reclaiming the coveted World Heavyweight Championship.

Before the ring announcer could even introduce Kane at *Night of Champions*, Undertaker made a beeline toward his brother, attacking him in the aisle. Contested under no-holds-barred rules, the match spent a considerable amount of time outside the ring before finally making its way into the ring.

Regardless of the locale, however, Undertaker had trouble getting the upper hand on Kane throughout, despite The Phenom's pre-match attack. Many speculated that Undertaker wasn't yet at one hundred percent after being put into a vegetative state months earlier, while others credited Kane's new ruthless attitude. Whatever the case, The Deadman did not look himself.

Late in the match, Undertaker found the strength to lift his brother up for the Tombstone, but he just couldn't seal the deal. Kane quickly reversed the move into a Tombstone of his own. A three count later, and the Big Red Machine had defeated The Deadman, emerging from his brother's mighty shadow in the process.

HELL IN A CELL

After defeating Undertaker at *Night of Champions*, Kane declared that the ring was now *his* yard, not his brother's. And with him now in charge, the Big Red Monster decided that he would end Undertaker once and for all inside Hell in a Cell, the same structure where Kane left his brother a mangled mess back in 1997.

Given Undertaker's uncharacteristic performance at *Night of Champions*, many fans wondered if climbing inside the satanic structure with Kane was a good idea. But then, out of nowhere, Paul Bearer shockingly returned to the side of The Phenom. Apparently putting their past troubles behind them, Bearer gave Undertaker the confidence he and the fans needed heading into Hell in a Cell.

Prior to the match starting, Bearer begged Undertaker to let him watch the match from within the Cell. But the request fell on deaf ears, as The Phenom escorted his longtime friend and manager outside the Cell to relative safety. The move proved wise; within seconds of the Cell door closing, Undertaker and Kane engaged in one of the most physical Hell in a Cell matches in recent memory.

Late in the contest, Kane countered an Undertaker Tombstone into one of his own, just as he did at *Night of Champions*. This time, however, Undertaker kicked out at two. Enraged over not being able to put The Deadman away, Kane inexplicably knocked the referee out cold.

Paramedics and officials quickly opened the Cell door and rushed to the referee's aid. While doing so, Paul Bearer was finally granted his wish when he slyly slipped into the Cell while the door was open. And once inside, Bearer finally revealed why he wanted in so badly.

Undertaker looked well on his way to certain victory when he lifted Kane for the Tombstone. But before The Phenom could drive his brother to the mat, Bearer intentionally blinded The Deadman with an otherwordly light from inside the urn. The manager then handed the urn to Kane, who used it to flatten Undertaker before hitting the Chokeslam for the win.

After committing the ultimate act of treason, a smiling Paul Bearer left by the side of his son, Kane, while Undertaker was left to assess what had just happened.

BURYING THE DEADMAN

Despite Kane already defeating Undertaker inside Hell in a Cell, Paul Bearer offered The Deadman yet another opportunity at the Big Red Monster's World Heavyweight Championship. And this time, Bearer upped the ante when he challenged Undertaker to the most macabre match in WWE history, a Buried Alive Match. Dying to get his hands on his brother again, The Deadman accepted, sans any signs of hesitation.

Having participated in all four Buried Alive Matches up to that point, Undertaker appeared to have the edge on paper. But any time the underhanded Paul Bearer is involved, things are rarely as they seem. And this match was no different, particularly toward the end.

With both Undertaker and Kane battling atop the gravesite, The Deadman was able to slip his signature Hell's Gate onto his brother. The pain from the move incapacitated Kane to the point where Undertaker was able to easily roll him into the grave for the apparent win. But just burying his brother wasn't enough for Undertaker; he also wanted retribution from Bearer.

The Phenom grabbed his former friend and manager by the back of the head and rammed him into a pile of dirt. He then clutched Bearer by the neck, looking to Chokeslam him into the grave atop is son. But before he could complete the task, The Nexus came running from the back and attacked Undertaker from behind.

The Deadman put up a good fight, but the numbers game was simply too much to overcome. Soon Kane emerged from the grave and clobbered Undertaker with the urn.

The combination of the Nexus attack and Kane's use of the urn was enough to send Undertaker into the grave. Members of Nexus began to bury The Deadman, but Kane quickly shooed them away. Instead, he wanted to do the honors himself. And he wanted to do it as only he could. With Undertaker unconscious at the bottom of the grave, Kane slowly lifted his arms then slammed them down with great force. The move mystically set in motion the nearby bulldozer, which responded by dropping approximately one ton of dirt atop The Deadman.

Kane and Paul Bearer briefly celebrated their victory before heading to the back. An eerie silence fell over the crowd. But then, once it looked like all hope was lost, Undertaker's signature gong was heard throughout the darkened arena and a lightning bolt hit the tombstone. As the capacity crowd erupted in joy, Undertaker's symbol mysteriously appeared over the grave, as if to say the end had not yet come.

Undertaker's tattoos are just as synonymous with The Deadman as his unparalleled *WrestleMania* success. But when Undertaker first arrived on the scene, he sported no visible artwork.

Undertaker's now famous tattoos began to take shape on his right forearm.

After a brief union with Brother Love, Undertaker joined forces with Paul Bearer. Opposition trembled in fear as they looked down the aisle and over Bearer's shoulders to find the gigantic Deadman clad in a dark overcoat and grey gloves.

When Undertaker returned in the summer of 1994 after an absence of several months, he traded in his grey gloves and boots for a more menacing purple.

A 1995 attack at the hands of King Mabel crushed Undertaker's face, forcing The Phenom to wear a facial appliance for protection.

The ever-evolving Undertaker.

In 1996, Undertaker began sporting a teardrop under his right eye, and exchanged his traditional gear for an updated leather look.

While ruling over his Ministry of Darkness, a more sadistic Undertaker covered himself in black from head to toe.

Undertaker underwent a drastic change in 2000 when he abandoned his Deadman persona in favor of the motorcycle-riding American Bad Ass.

The drastic changes continued in late 2001 when Undertaker cut his signature long hair.

The Deadman returned in 2004 with Paul Bearer by his side.

More than fifteen years after his debut, Undertaker appears to be in the best shape of his life.

Undertaker unveils an intimidating close-cropped hairstyle at *WrestleMania XXVIII*.

Undertaker sported a large goatee and a Mohawk when he went into battle with Brock Lesnar at *WrestleMania 30*.

With a look reminiscent of the 2004 Deadman, Undertaker defeated Bray Wyatt at *WrestleMania 31*.

147

RIVAL: TRIPLE H

Lasting more than a decade, the Undertaker-Triple H rivalry will forever go down as one of the most historic in sports-entertainment history. In its nascent stages, the two Superstars battled for survival and ultimately supremacy over the WWE roster. But as time passed, as well as several *WrestleMania* encounters, the rivalry eventually grew into a physical clash for respect between two of sports-entertainment's greatest outlaws.

APRIL 1, 2001 - *WRESTLEMANIA X-SEVEN*
UNDERTAKER DEFEATED TRIPLE H

With wins over the likes of Stone Cold Steve Austin and The Rock, Triple H had every right to be confident in 2001. But that confidence quickly turned to cockiness when he openly bragged about beating every one of the fans' heroes. Every one but Undertaker.

"You ain't never beat me," Undertaker told The Game, as the two Superstars stood nose to nose. "And if you try me, I'll make you famous."

Taking the American Bad Ass's challenge, Triple H did indeed try Undertaker. In fact, The Game went so far as to destroy his rival's $35,000 motorcycle just days before *WrestleMania*.

With the destruction of his bike fresh on his mind, Undertaker went right at Triple H well before the opening bell even rang, signifying that their *WrestleMania* encounter would be an all-out brawl. It was so intense, in fact, that the action eventually spilled out into the Astrodome crowd.

Battling among the masses, Undertaker and The Game eventually fought their way to the technical area and atop several scaffolds high above the stadium floor. Once there, the American Bad Ass Chokeslammed Triple H from the top of a camera tower all the way down to the floor. EMTs rushed to The Game's aid, but that didn't stop Undertaker from dropping an elbow on his opponent from atop the tower.

With the win in hand, Undertaker managed to get Triple H back in the ring, where he Tombstoned The Game for the apparent victory. But the referee was still down from an earlier attack. That didn't stop the American Bad Ass from continuing his assault, though. Undertaker lifted Triple H for the Last Ride, but while The Game was high in the air, he used his signature sledgehammer to flatten The Deadman. By this time the referee had recovered and began to count Undertaker's shoulders.

One, Two...Undertaker kicked out at the last moment. But Triple H smelled blood and continued his attack. With Undertaker in the corner, The Game climbed to the second rope and began unloading with a series of fists. The move looked good in theory, but it wasn't long before Undertaker lifted a vulnerably-positioned Game up for the Last Ride. This time, the impact of the move was enough to put Triple H away for good, extending Undertaker's *WrestleMania* undefeated streak to 9-0.

APRIL 3, 2011 - *WRESTLEMANIA XXVII*

UNDERTAKER DEFEATED TRIPLE H IN A NO HOLDS BARRED MATCH

In early 2011, mysterious videos began playing on WWE television that featured the numbers 2-21-11. Speculation immediately began to run rampant over the true meaning of the digits, but given the ominous nature of the videos, many excitedly assumed the numbers had something to do with Undertaker. And on February 21, 2011, those Deadman fans had their assumptions validated when after an extended absence, Undertaker finally reappeared on *Raw*.

Unfortunately for The Phenom, his return was quickly spoiled when Triple H made his way to the ring to confront him. Without saying a word, The Game walked right up to The Deadman, looked him in the eye, and then looked up at the *WrestleMania* sign hanging from the arena ceiling. Despite Triple H never opening his mouth, Undertaker, as well as the millions watching live, knew exactly what The Game wanted: a match at *WrestleMania XXVII*.

Undertaker simply smirked before ultimately performing his signature thumb-across-the-throat gesture, as if to say, "You're on." An excited Triple H responded with a D-Generation X crotch chop. Amazingly, the two Superstars' silence spoke volumes, as the entire sports-entertainment world immediately realized that two legends were set to square off at *WrestleMania*, despite neither ever uttering a word.

Within minutes of the opening bell, the no-holds-barred contest looked more like a demolition derby than a wrestling match. Both the Spanish and U.S. announce tables absorbed damage, as well as the nearby Cole Mine, where Michael Cole handled his commentating duties earlier in the evening.

When the match finally found its way back inside the ring, both Superstars managed to hit their signature moves on several occasions, but despite the intense impact of the maneuvers, neither victim stayed down. In fact, Triple H even hit Undertaker with an amazing three Pedigrees. And each time, The Deadman found a way to get a shoulder up before the three count.

After Undertaker kicked out of the third Pedigree, a determined Triple H nailed The Deadman with a series of brutal shots. "Stay down," The Game yelled. But Undertaker failed to heed his advice. Instead, he slowly got back up before ultimately being knocked back down again.

"Stay down; what is wrong with you?" Triple H screamed before nailing Undertaker with his own version of the Tombstone. Amazingly, however, not even the Tombstone could put The Deadman down. So as desperation set in, The Game went for his old, reliable sledgehammer.

"It's time," Triple H said as he prepared to crush Undertaker with the weapon. But before he could seal the deal, Undertaker used his very last ounce of energy to grab The Game and pull him into the Hell's Gate submission move. Triple H tried to escape for several moments, but in the end, the pressure was too much, forcing The Game to tap out.

With the win, Undertaker advanced his *WrestleMania* undefeated streak to 19-0, but judging from the post-match scenery, nobody would've known it. While a ravaged Triple H was able to slowly make his way to the back, Undertaker could barely move. He eventually tried to get to his feet, but the beating he absorbed had finally taken its toll. The WWE medical staff had no choice but to carry the victorious Undertaker out on a stretcher.

OTHER NOTABLE MATCHES:

- **June 25, 2000, *King of the Ring*:** Undertaker, Kane, and The Rock defeat WWE Champion Triple H, Shane McMahon, and Mr. McMahon.

- **June 23, 2002, *King of the Ring*:** Undisputed WWE Champion Undertaker defeats Triple H.

- **April 1, 2012, *WrestleMania XXVIII*:** Undertaker defeats Triple H.

UNDERTAKER VS. TRIPLE H

Date:	April 1, 2012
Event:	*WrestleMania XXVIII*
City:	Miami, Florida
Venue:	Sun Life Stadium
Commentators:	Michael Cole, Jim Ross, Jerry "The King" Lawler
Special Guest Referee:	Shawn Michaels

HELL IN A CELL

"You won the battle; I won the war," Triple H told Undertaker.

They were bold words for a man who had fallen short in his quest to defeat The Deadman at *WrestleMania XXVII*. But they were also words of truth. Even Undertaker agreed. Despite making The Game tap out, The Phenom claimed his life was a living hell following the victory, saying he continually re-lived in his mind the beating he took at the hands of Triple H. A beating that left Undertaker unable to leave the ring under his own cognizance.

Unwilling to let the sight of him being stretchered out be the lasting image people remember, Undertaker challenged Triple H to yet another match at *WrestleMania XXVIII*. But The Game denied The Deadman's request. So Undertaker turned to Plan B and pushed the one button he knew would get Triple H to accept.

"You know what, Hunter," started Undertaker. "You know that you can't do what your buddy, Shawn Michaels, couldn't do because Shawn was always better than you."

Undertaker's statement didn't sit well with Triple H, who in a moment of emotionally-fueled rage, quickly accepted The Phenom's challenge. Only this time, unlike the previous year's match, the two would battle within the confines of Hell in a Cell. Additionally, it was announced that Shawn Michaels would serve as special guest referee.

As expected, the match was a physical and emotional rollercoaster for all involved, including HBK, who was put in perhaps the most difficult situation of any official in WWE history. In one corner was Undertaker, a man Michaels respected tremendously. And in the other was his best friend, Triple H.

Numerous times throughout the contest, a conflicted HBK struggled with what was the right way to call the match. At one point, Undertaker absorbed so much steel from a near-countless number of blows from The Game that Michaels begged Triple H to stop. Not sharing HBK's compassion for the downed Deadman, Triple H refused. Instead, The Game told Michaels to end the match or else he'd end Undertaker once and for all.

HBK pleaded with The Phenom. But Undertaker refused to let Michaels call the match off. After several moments, The Deadman finally reached his feet, only to be flattened again, this time by a sledgehammer. The Game looked to land yet another sledgehammer shot, but Michaels wouldn't allow it, pulling the weapon from his friend's hands.

A concerned HBK leaned in to check on Undertaker, but surprisingly was put into Hell's Gate as he inched closer. The Deadman's motives were unclear. Perhaps he thought Michaels was Triple H. Or maybe he wanted to take the official out of the equation. Regardless, HBK was downed by the devastating maneuver.

Undertaker's attack on Michaels produced immediate consequences. Shortly after taking HBK out, The Phenom forced Triple H to nearly pass out to the Hell's Gate. But with Michaels still suffering from the effects of his own Hell's Gate, there was no referee to call for the bell.

When HBK finally recovered, he returned the favor to Undertaker, flattening him with Sweet Chin Music. Triple H then nailed The Deadman with the Pedigree. It appeared as though The Streak was finally coming to an end. But miraculously, Undertaker was able to kick out at two.

Michaels retreated to the corner and tucked his head in his hands. An internal struggle over how to best call the match was clearly rushing over him. But while HBK was an emotional wreck in the corner, Undertaker and Triple H were physical wrecks in the middle of the ring. However, that didn't stop them from continuing their battle.

Mirroring the earlier attack he suffered, Undertaker unleashed a series of relentless shots to Triple H. The attack was so brutal that HBK eventually turned his back, unable to watch the vicious attack.

The assault continued with Undertaker hitting The Game with his own sledgehammer before finally putting him away with a Tombstone. With the win, The Phenom extended his *WrestleMania* undefeated streak to an astounding 20-0.

Undertaker struggled to get up after the match. After several failed attempts, Michaels reached out and helped the war-torn Deadman to his feet. All the while, Triple H lay motionless in the center of the ring. In a situation eerily similar to *WrestleMania XXVII*, The Game was unable to leave the stadium on his own. It was at this moment that one of the most surreal images in sports-entertainment history took place. After more than thirty minutes of Hell, Undertaker and HBK put their arms around Triple H and helped him up the aisle.

Once at the top of the ramp, the three competitors showed the ultimate sign of respect for each other by sharing an emotional embrace that will live on as one of the most heartfelt moments in *WrestleMania* history.

RIVALS

For over a quarter of a century, dozens of Superstars have tried their hands at Undertaker, hoping they could be *the one* to finally make The Deadman rest in peace. But regardless of the size, fame, or past successes of these men, none have been able to solve the ominous figure that is the Undertaker.

HULK HOGAN

Perhaps Undertaker's first true great rival, Hulk Hogan has the unfortunate distinction of being the victim of The Phenom's first and fourth WWE Championship reigns. In between bookending title reigns, Undertaker and The Hulkster also ran into each other at *This Tuesday in Texas* when Hogan ended The Deadman's first WWE Championship reign. Additionally, Hogan eliminated Undertaker from the 1992 *Royal Rumble* Match.

YOKOZUNA

In addition to a pair of well-publicized Casket Matches in 1994, Undertaker and Yokozuna found themselves on opposite sides of the ring when The Deadman teamed with Lex Luger and the Steiners to battle Ludvig Borga, Jacques, Crush, and the nearly six-hundred-pound star from the Land of the Rising Sun at *Survivor Series*. Neither Undertaker nor Yokozuna were able to survive the traditional elimination match, as both were counted out while brawling outside the ring.

TED DIBIASE

Not long after introducing Undertaker to WWE, Ted DiBiase actually set out on a plan to rid the sports-entertainment scene of The Deadman. The Million Dollar Man tapped all his resources in an attempt to accomplish his goal, including calling on King Kong Bundy, Kama, Irwin R. Schyster, and a faux Undertaker. But despite his best efforts, DiBiase was never able to bury The Deadman.

BRET HART

Bret Hart and Undertaker faced off for the WWE Championship on many occasions, including the 1996 *Royal Rumble*, a February 1996 *Raw*, and *In Your House: Final Four*. But perhaps the most memorable confrontation came at *SummerSlam 1997* when, with the help of special guest referee Shawn Michaels, the "Hit Man" defeated The Deadman for the WWE Championship in controversial fashion.

SYCHO SID

When one promotion has two skyscrapers such as Undertaker and Sid, they're bound to cross paths. And that's exactly what they did at *WrestleMania 13* when The Deadman topped Sid for his second WWE Championship.

The two managed to battle several more times over the years, with most matches ending in either disqualification or countout. One exception came on a June 1997 episode of *Raw* where Undertaker successfully retained his WWE Championship after defeating Sid following a Tombstone.

VADER

With the sinister Paul Bearer leading the way, Vader was able to turn back Undertaker at the 1997 *Royal Rumble*. But in subsequent months, Vader failed to repeat his success, most notably at *In Your House: Canadian Stampede*, where Undertaker successfully defended his WWE Championship against the mighty Mastodon.

KING MABEL

In October 1995, King Mabel successfully pulled off what so many before him could never do when he knocked Undertaker out of action thanks to literally crushing The Phenom's face with a series of legdrops and headbutts. Mabel celebrated his accomplishment with great arrogance; but he would soon learn that incapacitating Undertaker comes with consequences. First, The Deadman and his team of Savio Vega, Henry Godwinn, and Fatu shutout Mabel, Isaac Yankem, Hunter Hearst-Helmsley, and Jerry Lawler at *Survivor Series*. Then in December 1995, Undertaker finished Mabel off when he convincingly defeated the King in a Casket Match at *In Your House: Season Beatings*.

DIESEL

Just when it looked like Undertaker would defeat Bret Hart for the WWE Championship at the 1996 *Royal Rumble*, in came Diesel, who pulled the referee out of the ring, causing a disqualification and setting off a brief but bitter rivalry with The Deadman. Undertaker quickly responded by ruining Diesel's WWE Championship opportunity at *In Your House: Rage in the Cage*, when The Phenom tore through the bottom of the mat and pulled Big Daddy Cool down under the ring with him. Then at *WrestleMania XII*, Undertaker defeated Diesel to extend his fledgling *WrestleMania* undefeated streak to 5-0.

THE ROCK

The Rock is a man that Undertaker both won tag team gold with *and* lost tag team gold to. But their tag team encounters are just a portion of the amazing history The Phenom and The Great One share, a history that includes multiple battles over the WWE Championship. Perhaps their most memorable clash over the title came at *Vengeance 2002* when The Rock won Undertaker's WWE Championship in a Triple Threat Match that also featured Kurt Angle. The only catch was that Undertaker wasn't even involved in the decision; Rock covered Angle for the win and the gold.

KURT ANGLE

When Kurt Angle poured milk on Undertaker's new Titan motorcycle, he knew he was about to become the American Bad Ass's chief target. So to make amends, Angle decided to present Undertaker with a new bike. Only this bike was nothing like the Titan motorcycle; instead, Angle presented Undertaker with a little white scooter.

The series of ill-advised moves by Angle launched an on-again off-again rivalry that lasted more than half a decade. Perhaps the most memorable battle between the two took place at *Survivor Series 2000* when Angle controversially retained his WWE Championship by employing the help of his lookalike brother, Eric.

JBL

When Bradshaw was taking orders from Undertaker as part of The Deadman's Ministry of Darkness, few thought the beer-swilling Texan would one day transform himself into a main event player. But that's exactly what happened years later when JBL began to flaunt his wealth. The self-made millionaire soon had the confidence to shoot straight to the top of the card and eventually become WWE Champion. And with such prestige, as almost all main eventers eventually realize, came the unfortunate fact that he must cross paths with Undertaker.

Luckily for JBL, he managed to eke by The Deadman each time with his championship reign intact. Most famously, JBL defeated Undertaker at *SummerSlam 2004* when The Phenom was disqualified for using the title as a weapon. Later at *No Mercy*, JBL got lucky again when Heidenreich's interference allowed the champ to get the win over Undertaker in a Last Ride Match.

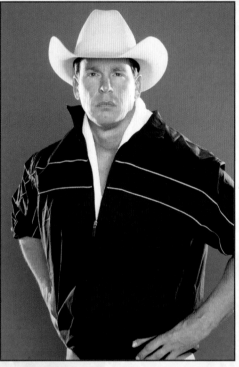

BIG SHOW

Two World Tag Team Championship reigns with Big Show were not enough to keep Undertaker and The World's Largest Athlete from also being heated rivals at various points over the years. The duo's first big rivalry came in 2003 when Big Show began giving The Deadman a series of mysterious gifts, including a puppy and Brother Love. In reality, the presents were designed to be a distraction so Big Show could attack Undertaker from behind, which he did on a February edition of *SmackDown*.

Ultimately, Big Show's gamesmanship proved to be a poor tactical error, as Undertaker went on to defeat The World's Largest Athlete in a series of high-profile matches, including *No Way Out 2003* and *WrestleMania XIX*, where Big Show teamed with A-Train.

Show earned a measure of revenge years later when he defeated Undertaker at *No Mercy 2008*. But that victory was quickly followed by another series of high-profile losses to Undertaker, this time in a Last Man Standing Match at *Cyber Sunday 2008* and a Casket Match at *Survivor Series 2008*.

MARK HENRY

Mark Henry had a way of ruining championship matches for Undertaker over the years. First in March 2006, the World's Strongest Man interfered in The Deadman's World Heavyweight Championship Match with Kurt Angle, slamming The Phenom through the announce table in the process. And in the following year, Henry attacked an already battered Undertaker from behind, leaving him nearly motionless and easy pickings for Mr. Money in the Bank, Edge, to swoop in and defeat The Phenom for the World Heavyweight Title. While both cases were certainly setbacks for Undertaker, he made sure revenge would eventually come Henry's way. In 2006, The Deadman defeated the World's Strongest Man in a Casket Match at *WrestleMania 22*. And in the following year, *Unforgiven 2007* served as the site of Undertaker's retribution, as he beat Henry in the night's main event.

THE GREAT KHALI

Few Superstars have made as impactful a debut as The Great Khali, who attacked an unsuspecting Undertaker in his first-ever WWE appearance. At seven-foot-one, Khali appeared to be the one Superstar who could finally rid WWE of Undertaker. And at *Judgment Day 2006*, he went a long way toward accomplishing that feat, defeating The Deadman in under ten minutes. Things looked bleak for Undertaker, but in typical Phenom fashion, he battled back and eventually proved his superiority over Khali in a Last Man Standing Match on *SmackDown*.

BATISTA

The only thing fans knew for sure when Undertaker won the 2007 Royal Rumble Match was that The Phenom was guaranteed an opportunity at the championship of his choosing at *WrestleMania 23*. What they didn't realize was that when The Deadman chose to go after Batista, it set off a yearlong rivalry over one of the most prestigious prizes in sports-entertainment history, the World Heavyweight Championship. The initial battle took place at *WrestleMania 23*, where Undertaker not only captured The Animal's World Heavyweight Title, but also extended his winning streak to 15-0.

Throughout the rest of the year, Undertaker and Batista main evented show after show, each battling for the right to be called World Heavyweight Champion. The intense rivalry eventually reached its conclusion in November when Batista defeated Undertaker in a Hell in a Cell Match at *Survivor Series*, thanks in large part to interference by Edge.

EDGE

The Edge-Undertaker rivalry initially revolved around a shared desire to be World Heavyweight Champion, but was ultimately marred by the controversial decisions of *SmackDown* General Manager Vickie Guerrero. After losing the title to Undertaker in the main event of *WrestleMania XXIV*, Edge was granted his rematch at *Backlash*. Unfortunately for the Rated-R Superstar, he lost that match as well, this time by submission. With the victory, Undertaker appeared to have Edge out of his way, but Guerrero soon emerged and used her power to strip The Deadman of the gold, claiming the submission move he used on Edge was illegal.

Even more shenanigans prevented Undertaker from winning the title back at *Judgment Day*. But The Phenom eventually gained retribution against Edge when he defeated the Rated-R Superstar in an excruciating Hell in a Cell match at *SummerSlam 2008*.

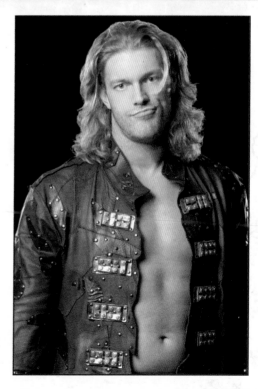

THE STREAK DIES

In February 2014, Paul Heyman lobbied for his client, Brock Lesnar, to receive a WWE World Heavyweight Championship opportunity at *WrestleMania 30*. Instead, what The Authority gave Heyman was an open contract for his client to face any Superstar of their choosing at the annual spectacular. Despite the near endless opportunities the open contract represented, they declined, calling the proposal unacceptable.

Upset over not getting their championship match, Heyman and Lesnar began to leave the ring. But before they could get too far, the familiar sound of Undertaker's gong rang through the arena, stopping the duo in their tracks.

Once in the ring, Undertaker walked right up to Lesnar and stood nose to nose with him. The Deadman then looked up at the *WrestleMania* sign, insinuating that he wanted The Beast on the biggest stage of them all.

Despite appearing slightly unnerved, Lesnar signed the contract. But when it came time for Undertaker's signature, The Deadman didn't move. Heyman barked at him to sign the document, but that did little to move The Phenom. Lesnar then put his palm on the contract and demanded The Deadman put his signature down. So he did. But he did it his way, by ramming the pen through Lesnar's hand, then Chokeslamming The Beast through the table set up in the ring. With that, what would turn out to be one of the most history-altering matches of all time was set in stone: Undertaker versus Brock Lesnar at *WrestleMania 30*.

In Memory of
WILLIAM MOODY
"PAUL BEARER"
1954 - 2013

When Paul Bearer passed away in March 2013, CM Punk saw an opening that no other Superstar had before. Dripping with disrespect, Punk continually mocked the recently deceased manager, stole his urn, and even interrupted a ceremony in Bearer's honor. The Straight Edge Superstar's actions were designed to expose Undertaker's emotions and take him off his game heading into *WrestleMania 29*. But what he learned once the bell rang was that it did nothing more than motivate The Phenom, who defeated Punk to go 21-0 at *WrestleMania* and more importantly, properly honor his longtime friend.

When a heavy-hearted Undertaker defeated CM Punk at *WrestleMania 29*, it seemed as though The Streak would never end. Many of sports-entertainment's biggest names tried their hand at ending The Deadman, including Ric Flair, Randy Orton, Edge, Batista, Triple H, and Shawn Michaels, but none of them could pull it off.

Was there no man that could defeat The Deadman at *WrestleMania*? Maybe not. But there certainly was a Beast.

In the weeks leading up to *WrestleMania*, Lesnar threatened to "Eat, Sleep, Conquer, Repeat" Undertaker's remarkable streak. And once the opening bell rang, his threat proved to be so much more than just a catchphrase on a T-shirt, as The Beast owned Undertaker throughout much of the match's early goings. Amazingly, however, The Deadman somehow found the strength to fight back and eventually nail Lesnar with a Chokeslam.

Unfortunately for Undertaker, the Chokeslam failed to defeat The Beast. Even worse, The Phenom followed up with a series of signature moves that were ultimately countered by Lesnar. First, Undertaker lifted The Beast for what appeared to be a Tombstone. But before The Deadman could land the move, Lesnar reversed it into a devastating F-5. Later, Undertaker attempted Old School, but was met with another F-5 prior to executing the maneuver.

Amazingly, Undertaker was able to withstand both F-5s, and was even able to recover and nail Lesnar with a Tombstone. A twenty-second straight *WrestleMania* victory appeared just moments away. Undertaker symbolically placed The Beast's arms across his chest and went for the pin. But before the referee could complete the three count, Lesnar miraculously got a shoulder up.

A wide-eyed Undertaker struggled to comprehend what had just happened. Once it registered, however, The Phenom set out to destroy Lesnar for good with yet another Tombstone. This time, though, the move that had carried Undertaker to so many *WrestleMania* victories was reversed into yet another F-5.

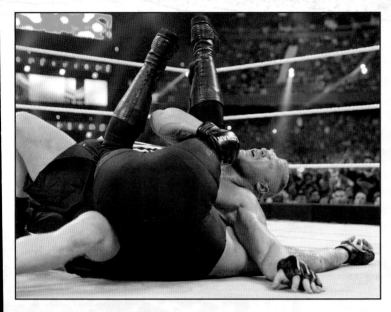

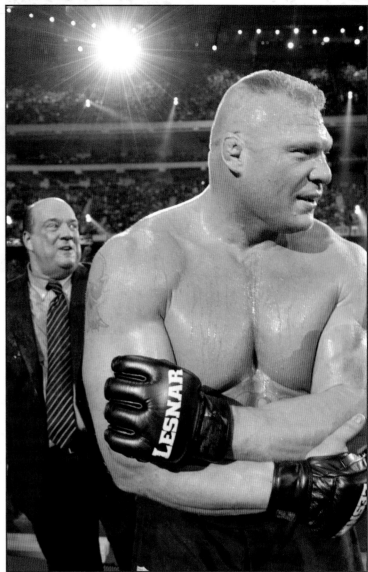

Undertaker's epic *WrestleMania* undefeated streak had been served its last rites, as three F-5s ultimately proved too much for The Deadman to overcome. The referee counted to three and a stunned silence overcame the capacity crowd as they struggled to assess what they had just witnessed. The greatest streak in the history of sports-entertainment had just been crushed.

As Lesnar and Heyman gloated all the way up the ramp, Undertaker struggled to get to his feet. Once up, though, The Deadman was met with a deserving standing ovation. Chants of "Undertaker" rang out, as the crowd paid respect to the greatest performer in *WrestleMania* history.

With the victory, Lesnar not only proved Undertaker's mortality, but he also cemented himself as one of the greatest competitors in WWE history. As "the one" in 21-1, The Beast employed a never-before-seen brand of dominance to catapult himself straight to the top of the marquee. And within months, Lesnar had soundly defeated John Cena to become perhaps the most feared WWE World Heavyweight Champion in history.

RESURRECTION OF THE DEADMAN

After Undertaker's shocking defeat at the hands of Brock Lesnar at *WrestleMania 30*, many questioned if The Deadman would ever show his face again. But as *WrestleMania 31* neared, one man made it his mission to lure Undertaker back to WWE. That man was Bray Wyatt.

In early 2015, Wyatt released a series of cryptic messages that left many scratching their heads. By the tenor of the communications, it was clear The Eater of Worlds had his sights set on somebody of incredible stature, but it wasn't entirely clear where the target was pointing. That was until *Fastlane* when Wyatt revealed his prey in the most derisive way.

With a crew of torch-carrying druids leading the way, a casket was slowly delivered to ringside. Many watching *Fastlane* assumed a returning Undertaker was inside, but once the top was opened, it was Wyatt who emerged with a menacing grin on his face.

"I want you to know that I don't fear you anymore," said Wyatt. "I am pain. I am suffering. I am Bray Wyatt, the new face of fear! And at *WrestleMania*, I will claim the soul of the Undertaker."

With that, Wyatt's mission was clear; he planned to make *WrestleMania 31* The Deadman's final resting place. But despite Wyatt's goading, Undertaker never responded to the challenge, forcing The Eater of Worlds to continue his crusade to call out The Phenom.

Wyatt's campaign climaxed weeks later on *Raw* when he mockingly opened Undertaker's urn, which he disrespectfully called a jar, and laughed upon finding nothing inside. Moments later, however, smoke began to mysteriously emerge from the urn, as Undertaker's signature gong rang out throughout the arena. Then, from out of nowhere, Wyatt's once-destroyed rocking chair appeared in perfect condition in the middle of the ring.

Wyatt looked around feverishly, but Undertaker was nowhere to be found. His presence, however, was undeniable, as the TitanTron above the entranceway displayed a message for Wyatt: At *WrestleMania*, the man comes around.

Undertaker wasn't done yet. After accepting the challenge, a bolt of lightning shot down from the heavens and struck Wyatt's rocking chair, setting it ablaze. Flames rippled through the air, while Wyatt laughed maniacally, realizing he had finally received the answer for which he had been yearning.

Given Undertaker's track record at *WrestleMania*, many thought Wyatt was crazy to call out the illustrious event's greatest competitor. Twenty-one times sports-entertainment's greatest names tried to vanquish The Deadman, and twenty-one times they were buried. And as the event neared, fans everywhere questioned why Wyatt thought he could do what Triple H, Shawn Michaels, Ric Flair, and so many others couldn't.

Despite The Deadman's success at *WrestleMania*, Wyatt showed no fear of being in the same ring with the event's greatest legend. And at one point, he even mocked Undertaker by performing The Phenom's signature thumb-across-the-throat gesture before attempting Sister Abigail. The cockiness, however, proved costly, as it allowed Undertaker to recover and counter into a Chokeslam.

Following the Chokeslam, Undertaker nailed Wyatt with a Tombstone and went for the pin. It seemed The Deadman had regained his *WrestleMania* swagger, as an apparent victory was mere moments away. Amazingly, however, Wyatt kicked out prior to the three count.

Undertaker collapsed in disbelief, while fans everywhere began to question if Wyatt truly was the new face of fear. Only the absolute elite have ever kicked out of the Tombstone, and now Wyatt was a member of that elusive club.

The Deadman eventually collected himself and went for another Tombstone. This time, however, it was countered into Sister Abigail. The end appeared near. Undertaker, many assumed, was about to go out on his shield, perhaps never to be seen again. But before those assumptions could become reality, The Phenom kicked out at two.

An agitated Wyatt proceeded to go at Undertaker at a furious pace. He then went for a second Sister Abigail. And this time, he attempted to seal the deal with a kiss to The Deadman's forehead. In the end, though, the gesture proved to be the kiss of death for Wyatt, as Undertaker countered Sister Abigail into a Tombstone for the win. With the victory, The Phenom improved his incredible *WrestleMania* record to 22-1, and, more importantly, proved that he would not go quietly into the night.

PAY-PER-VIEW HISTORY

1990 1991

11 / 22 / 1990

Survivor Series: ▶
Undertaker
eliminated from
Survivor Series
Elimination Match
via countout.

1 / 19 / 1991

◀ ***Royal Rumble:*** The Legion of Doom eliminated Undertaker from the Royal Rumble Match.

3 / 24 / 1991

WrestleMania VII: Undertaker ▶ defeated Jimmy "Superfly" Snuka.

11 / 27 / 1991

◀ ***Survivor Series:*** Undertaker defeated Hulk Hogan for the WWE Championship.

1 / 19 / 1992

Royal Rumble: Hulk Hogan eliminated Undertaker from the Royal Rumble Match.

1992

12 / 3 / 1991

◀ ***This Tuesday in Texas:*** Hulk Hogan defeated Undertaker for the WWE Championship.

4 / 5 / 1992

WrestleMania VIII: Undertaker defeated Jake "The Snake" Roberts. ▼

8 / 31 / 1992

SummerSlam: Undertaker defeated Kamala via disqualification.

1993

11 / 25 / 1992

Survivor Series: Undertaker defeated Kamala (Coffin Match).

1 / 24 / 1993

Royal Rumble: An interfering Giant Gonzales eliminated Undertaker from the Royal Rumble Match.

4 / 4 / 1993

WrestleMania IX: Undertaker defeated Giant Gonzales via disqualification.

11 / 24 / 1993

Survivor Series: ▶ Undertaker eliminated from Survivor Series Elimination Match via countout.

11 / 23 / 1994

Survivor Series: ▶ Undertaker defeated Yokozuna (Casket Match).

8 / 30 / 1993

SummerSlam: Undertaker defeated Giant Gonzales (Rest in Peace Match).

1994 ◆ ◆ ◆ 1995 ◆ ◆

8 / 29 / 1994

SummerSlam: Undertaker defeated Undertaker.

1 / 22 / 1994

Royal Rumble: WWE Champion Yokozuna defeated Undertaker (Casket Match).

1 / 22 / 1995

Royal Rumble: Undertaker defeated Irwin R. Schyster.

4 / 2 / 1995

WrestleMania XI: Undertaker defeated King Kong Bundy.

1 / 21 / 1996

◄ *Royal Rumble*: Undertaker defeated WWE Champion Bret Hart via disqualification.

3 / 31 / 1996

WrestleMania XII: Undertaker defeated Diesel.

6 / 2 / 1995

King of the Ring: Mabel defeated Undertaker (King of the Ring quarterfinals).

8 / 27 / 1995

SummerSlam: Undertaker defeated Kama (Casket Match).

1996

11 / 19 / 1995

Survivor Series: Undertaker, Henry Godwinn, Savio Vega, and Fatu defeated Jerry Lawler, Isaac Yankem, King Mabel, and Hunter Hearst-Helmsley (Survivor Series Elimination Match).

12 / 17 / 1995

In Your House: Seasons Beatings: Undertaker defeated King Mabel (Casket Match).

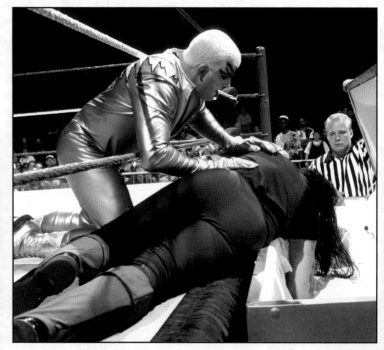

5 / 28 / 1996

In Your House: Beware of Dog: Intercontinental Champion Goldust defeated Undertaker (Casket Match).

8 / 18 / 1996

SummerSlam: Mankind defeated Undertaker (Boiler Room Brawl).

7 / 21 / 1996

In Your House: International Incident: Undertaker defeated Goldust via disqualification.

6 / 23 / 1996

King of the Ring: Mankind defeated Undertaker.

9 / 21 / 1996

In Your House: Mind Games: Undertaker defeated Goldust (Final Curtain Match).

10 / 20 / 1996

In Your House: Buried Alive: Undertaker defeated Mankind (Buried Alive Match).

11 / 17 / 1996

Survivor Series: Undertaker defeated Mankind.

12 / 15 / 1996

In Your House: It's Time: Undertaker defeated The Executioner (Armageddon Rules Match).

2 / 16 / 1997

In Your House: Final Four: Bret Hart defeated Undertaker, Vader, and Stone Cold Steve Austin for the vacant WWE Championship (Four Corners Elimination Match).

1 / 19 / 1997

Royal Rumble: Vader defeated Undertaker.

4 / 20 / 1997

In Your House: Revenge of the Taker: WWE Champion Undertaker defeated Mankind.

1997

1 / 19 / 1997

Royal Rumble: Stone Cold Steve Austin eliminated Undertaker from the Royal Rumble Match.

5 / 11 / 1997

In Your House: A Cold Day in Hell: WWE Champion Undertaker defeated Stone Cold Steve Austin.

3 / 23 / 1997

WrestleMania 13: Undertaker defeated Sycho Sid for the WWE Championship.

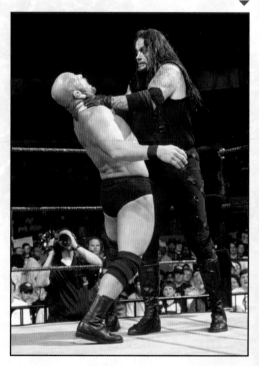

King of the Ring: WWE Champion Undertaker defeated Faarooq.

7 / 6 / 1997

In Your House: Canadian Stampede: WWE Champion Undertaker defeated Vader.

8 / 3 / 1997

SummerSlam: Bret Hart ▶ defeated Undertaker for the WWE Championship.

9 / 7 / 1997

In Your House: Ground Zero: Undertaker versus Shawn Michaels ended in a no-contest.

10 / 5 / 1997

◀ *In Your House: Badd Blood:* Shawn Michaels defeated Undertaker (Hell in a Cell).

12 / 7 / 1997

In Your House: D-Generation X: Jeff Jarrett defeated Undertaker via disqualification.

1 / 18 / 1998

Royal Rumble: WWE Champion Shawn Michaels defeated Undertaker (Casket Match).

4 / 26 / 1998

In Your House: Unforgiven: ▶ Undertaker defeated Kane (Inferno Match).

3 / 29 / 1998

WrestleMania XIV: Undertaker defeated Kane.

1998

6 / 28 / 1998

King of the Ring: Undertaker defeated Mankind (Hell in a Cell).

7 / 26 / 1998

◀ *In Your House: Fully Loaded:* Undertaker and Stone Cold Steve Austin defeated Kane and Mankind for the World Tag Team Championship.

8 / 30 / 1998

SummerSlam: WWE Champion Stone Cold Steve Austin defeated Undertaker.

9 / 27 / 1998

In Your House: Breakdown: Undertaker and Kane defeated WWE Champion Stone Cold Steve Austin (Triple Threat Match).

10 / 18 / 1998

In Your House: Judgment Day: Undertaker versus Kane ended in a no-contest.

11 / 15 / 1998

Survivor Series: Undertaker defeated Kane (WWE Championship tournament quarterfinals).

11 / 15 / 1998

◄ *Survivor Series*: The Rock defeated Undertaker via disqualification (WWE Championship tournament semifinals).

12 / 13 / 1998

In Your House: Rock Bottom: Stone Cold Steve Austin defeated Undertaker (Buried Alive Match).

3 / 28 / 1999

WrestleMania XV:
Undertaker defeated Big
Boss Man (Hell in a Cell).

5 / 23 / 1999

Over the Edge: Undertaker ▶
defeated Stone Cold Steve Austin
for the WWE Championship.

1999

4 / 25 / 1999

In Your House: Backlash:
Undertaker defeated
Ken Shamrock.

6 / 27 / 1999

King of the Ring: WWE
Champion Undertaker
defeated The Rock.

7 / 25 / 1999

Fully Loaded: WWE
Champion Stone Cold
Steve Austin defeated
Undertaker (First
Blood Match).

8 / 22 / 1999

SummerSlam: Undertaker and Big Show defeated Kane
and X-Pac for the World Tag Team Championship.

6 / 25 / 2000

King of the Ring: ▶
Undertaker, Kane, and
The Rock defeated
WWE Champion Triple
H, Shane McMahon,
and Mr. McMahon (The
Rock won the WWE
Championship).

7 / 23 / 2000

Fully Loaded: Undertaker defeated Kurt Angle.

11 / 19 / 2000

Survivor Series: WWE Champion Kurt Angle
defeated Undertaker.

2000

8 / 27 / 2000

SummerSlam:
Undertaker versus
Kane ended in a
no-contest.

9 / 24 / 2000

Unforgiven: WWE Champion The Rock
defeated Undertaker, Chris Benoit, and
Kane (Fatal Four Way Match). ▼

12 / 10 / 2000

Armageddon: WWE Champion Kurt Angle
defeated Undertaker, Stone Cold Steve Austin,
The Rock, Triple H, and Rikishi (Hell in a Cell). ▼

1 / 21 / 2001

Royal Rumble: Rikishi eliminated Undertaker from the Royal Rumble Match.

2 / 25 / 2001

No Way Out: World Tag Team Champions The Dudley Boyz defeated Undertaker and Kane, and Edge and Christian (Triple Threat Tables Match).

5 / 20 / 2001

Judgment Day: WWE Champion Stone Cold Steve Austin defeated Undertaker (No Holds Barred Match).

8 / 19 / 2001

SummerSlam: WCW Tag Team Champions Undertaker and Kane defeated Diamond Dallas Page and Kanyon for the World Tag Team Championship (Steel Cage Match).

2001

4 / 1 / 2001

WrestleMania X-Seven: Undertaker defeated Triple H.

7 / 22 / 2001

Invasion: Booker T, Diamond Dallas Page, Rhyno, and The Dudley Boyz defeated Undertaker, Kane, Stone Cold Steve Austin, Chris Jericho, and Kurt Angle.

4 / 29 / 2001

Backlash: WWE Champion Stone Cold Steve Austin and Intercontinental Champion Triple H defeated Undertaker and Kane for the World Tag Team Championship.

9 / 23 / 2001

Unforgiven: WCW Tag Team Champions Undertaker and Kane defeated Kronik.

10 / 21 / 2001

No Mercy: Undertaker defeated Booker T.

11 / 18 / 2001

Survivor Series: Undertaker ▶ eliminated from Survivor Series Elimination Match by Kurt Angle.

12 / 9 / 2001

◀ ***Vengeance:*** Undertaker defeated Rob Van Dam for the Hardcore Championship.

4 / 21 / 2002

Backlash: Undertaker defeated Stone Cold Steve Austin.

6 / 23 / 2002

King of the Ring: WWE Champion Undertaker defeated Triple H.

1 / 20 / 2002

Royal Rumble: Maven eliminated Undertaker from the Royal Rumble Match.

2 / 17 / 2002

No Way Out: The Rock defeated Undertaker.

2002

3 / 17 / 2002

WrestleMania X8: Undertaker defeated Ric Flair (No Disqualification Match).

5 / 19 / 2002

◄ *Judgment Day:* Undertaker defeated Hulk Hogan for the WWE Championship.

8 / 25 / 2002

SummerSlam: Undertaker
defeated Test.

10 / 20 / 2002

No Mercy: WWE Champion Brock Lesnar defeated
Undertaker (Hell in a Cell).

7 / 21 / 2002

◀ *Vengeance*: The Rock defeated Undertaker (c)
and Kurt Angle to win the WWE Championship
(Triple Threat Match).

9 / 22 / 2002

Unforgiven: WWE Champion Brock
Lesnar versus Undertaker ended in a
double disqualification.

177

Survivor Series: Kane laughs maniacally as Mr. McMahon defeated Undertaker (Buried Alive Match).

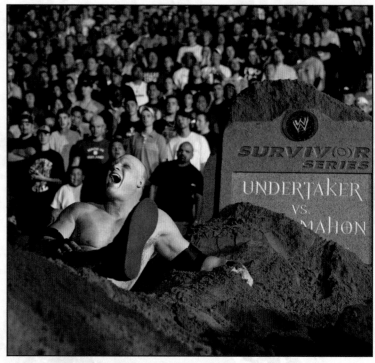

1 / 19 / 2003

Royal Rumble: Brock Lesnar eliminated Undertaker from the Royal Rumble Match.

3 / 30 / 2003

WrestleMania XIX: Undertaker defeated Big Show and A-Train (Handicap Match).

2003

2 / 23 / 2003

No Way Out: Undertaker defeated Big Show.

7 / 27 / 2003

Vengeance: Undertaker defeated John Cena.

10 / 19 / 2003

No Mercy: WWE Champion Brock Lesnar defeated Undertaker (Biker Chain Match).

8 / 24 / 2003

◄ **SummerSlam:** Undertaker defeated A-Train.

3 / 14 / 2004

◀ *WrestleMania XX*:
Undertaker defeated Kane.

7 / 27 / 2004

The Great American Bash: Undertaker
defeated The Dudley Boyz (Handicap Match).

2004

5 / 16 / 2004

Judgment Day: Undertaker
defeated Booker T.

8 / 25 / 2004

SummerSlam: WWE Champion JBL defeated
Undertaker via disqualification.

10 / 3 / 2004

No Mercy: WWE
Champion JBL
defeated Undertaker
(Last Ride Match).

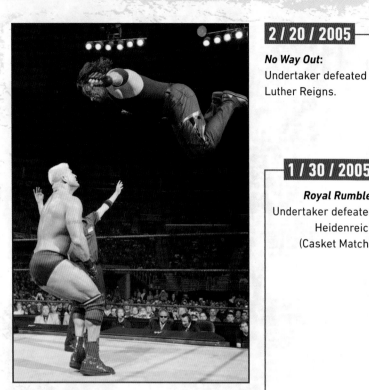

2 / 20 / 2005

No Way Out: Undertaker defeated Luther Reigns.

The Great American Bash: Undertaker defeated Muhammad Hassan.

1 / 30 / 2005

Royal Rumble: Undertaker defeated Heidenreich (Casket Match).

11 / 14 / 2004

Survivor Series: Undertaker defeated Heidenreich.

2005

11 / 12 / 2004

Armageddon: WWE Champion JBL defeated Undertaker, Booker T, and Eddie Guerrero (Fatal Four Way Match).

4 / 3 / 2005

WrestleMania 21: Undertaker defeated Randy Orton.

10 / 9 / 2005

No Mercy: Randy and "Cowboy" Bob Orton defeated Undertaker (Handicap Casket Match).

12 / 18 / 2005

Armageddon: ▶ Undertaker defeated Randy Orton (Hell in a Cell).

4 / 2 / 2006

WrestleMania 22: Undertaker defeated Mark Henry (Casket Match).

2006

8 / 21 / 2005

SummerSlam: Randy Orton defeated Undertaker.

2 / 19 / 2006

No Way Out: World Heavyweight Champion Kurt Angle defeated Undertaker.

5 / 21 / 2006

Judgment Day: The Great Khali defeated Undertaker.

1 / 28 / 2007

◄ *Royal Rumble*:
Undertaker won the
Royal Rumble Match.

10 / 8 / 2006

No Mercy: Mr. Kennedy defeated
Undertaker via disqualification.

12 / 17 / 2006

Armageddon: Undertaker
defeated Mr. Kennedy (Last
Ride Match).

2 / 18 / 2007

No Way Out: John Cena and Shawn
Michaels defeated Undertaker and Batista.

2007

11 / 26 / 2006

Survivor Series: Mr. Kennedy
defeated Undertaker (First
Blood Match).

7 / 23 / 2006

The Great American Bash:
Undertaker defeated Big Show
(Punjabi Prison Match).

4 / 1 / 2007

WrestleMania 23: Undertaker
defeated Batista for the World
Heavyweight Championship.

9 / 16 / 2007

Unforgiven: Undertaker defeated Mark Henry.

4 / 29 / 2007

Backlash: World Heavyweight Champion Undertaker versus Batista ended in a draw (Last Man Standing Match).

12 / 16 / 2007

Armageddon: Edge defeated Undertaker and Batista (c) for the World Heavyweight Championship (Triple Threat Match).

10 / 28 / 2007

◀ *Cyber Sunday:* World Heavyweight Champion Batista defeated Undertaker.

11 / 18 / 2007

Survivor Series: World Heavyweight Champion Batista defeated Undertaker (Hell in a Cell).

1 / 27 / 2008

Royal Rumble: Shawn Michaels eliminated Undertaker from the Royal Rumble Match.

2 / 17 / 2008

No Way Out: ▶ Undertaker defeated Batista, Montel Vontavious Porter, Big Daddy V, Finlay, and The Great Khali (Elimination Chamber Match).

◀ 1998

3 / 30 / 2008

WrestleMania XXIV: Undertaker defeated Edge for the World Heavyweight Championship.

4 / 27 / 2008

◀ *Backlash:* World Heavyweight Champion Undertaker defeated Edge.

Judgment Day: Undertaker defeated Edge via countout (World Heavyweight Championship Match for the vacant title).

6 / 1 / 2008

One Night Stand: Edge defeated Undertaker for the vacant World Heavyweight Championship (TLC Match).

8 / 17 / 2008

SummerSlam: Undertaker defeated Edge (Hell in a Cell).

10 / 5 / 2008

◄ *No Mercy:* Big Show defeated Undertaker.

10 / 26 / 2008

◄ *Cyber Sunday:* Undertaker defeated Big Show (Last Man Standing Match).

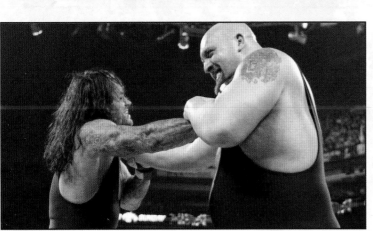

11 / 23 / 2008

Survivor Series: Undertaker defeated Big Show (Casket Match).

1 / 25 / 2009

Royal Rumble: Big Show eliminated Undertaker from the Royal Rumble Match.

4 / 5 / 2009

WrestleMania XXV: Undertaker ▶ defeated Shawn Michaels.

2009

2 / 15 / 2009

No Way Out: Triple H defeated Undertaker, Jeff Hardy, Big Show, Vladimir Kozlov, and Edge (c) for the WWE Championship (Elimination Chamber Match).

9 / 13 / 2009

WWE Breaking Point: World Heavyweight Champion CM Punk defeated Undertaker (Submission Match).

10 / 4 / 2009

Hell in a Cell: Undertaker defeated CM Punk for the World Heavyweight Championship (Hell in a Cell).

10 / 25 / 2009

WWE Bragging Rights: World Heavyweight Champion Undertaker defeated CM Punk, Rey Mysterio, and Batista (Fatal Four Way Match). ▼

11 / 22 / 2009

Survivor Series: ▶
World Heavyweight
Champion Undertaker
defeated Big Show
and Chris Jericho
(Triple Threat Match).

2 / 21 / 2010

Elimination Chamber: Chris Jericho defeated Undertaker (c), CM Punk, Rey Mysterio, John
Morrison, and R-Truth for the World Heavyweight Championship (Elimination Chamber Match).

2010

12 / 13 / 2009

WWE TLC: World
Heavyweight Champion
Undertaker defeated Batista
(Chairs Match).

1 / 31 / 2010

Royal Rumble: World Heavyweight
Champion Undertaker defeated
Rey Mysterio.
▼

3 / 28 / 2010

WrestleMania XXVI: Undertaker defeated
Shawn Michaels (Streak vs. Career Match).
▼

4 / 7 / 2013

WrestleMania 29: Undertaker defeated CM Punk.

4 / 1 / 2012

◄ **WrestleMania XXVIII**: Undertaker defeated Triple H (Hell in a Cell).

4 / 3 / 2011

WrestleMania XXVII: ► Undertaker defeated Triple H.

10 / 3 / 2010

Hell in a Cell: World Heavyweight Champion Kane defeated Undertaker (Hell in a Cell).

2011

2012

10 / 24 / 2010

WWE Bragging Rights: World ► Heavyweight Champion Kane defeated Undertaker (Buried Alive Match).

9 / 19 / 2010

Night of Champions: World Heavyweight Champion Kane defeated Undertaker (No Holds Barred Match).

4 / 6 / 2014

WrestleMania 30: Brock Lesnar defeated Undertaker to end The Streak.

2013

2014

2015

3 / 29 / 2015

WrestleMania 31: Undertaker defeated Bray Wyatt.

FOREVER A LEGEND

When Undertaker first appeared in WWE in November 1990, it was immediately evident that he was unlike any Superstar in history. Never before had one force combined such a chilling and ominous presence with foreboding size and superior athleticism. But despite The Deadman possessing so many incredible attributes at the time of his debut, not even the most educated sports-entertainment insider could've predicted the more than two decades of dominance that would follow.

Equipped with an unmatched ability to continually evolve, Undertaker has spent his twenty-plus years transforming from a menacing newcomer, to a main event Superstar, to a sadistic ringleader, to an American Bad Ass, and finally to one of the biggest legends of all time. And while change has played an integral role in The Deadman's ability to survive and thrive, there has always been one constant when it comes to Undertaker: the WWE ring is his yard and those daring enough to play in it will pay the consequences.

Along the way, Undertaker has complemented his legendary identity with an equally impressive list of in-ring accomplishments: WWE Champion, World Heavyweight Champion, World Tag Team Champion, Royal Rumble winner.... The list is nearly endless, and there are few—if any—that can match it. But even more impressive has been The Deadman's amazing success at *WrestleMania*.

With more than twenty victories to his credit, Undertaker has created a legacy that will never be duplicated. Others will find success at the Showcase of the Immortals, but only The Deadman will *forever* be synonymous with The Show of Shows. Generations from now, fans will still be buzzing about what Undertaker has been able to accomplish at *WrestleMania*. More than Hulk Hogan, Stone Cold Steve Austin, or John Cena, fans will forever associate the biggest event in live entertainment history with The Phenom.

And if *WrestleMania 31* has taught the world anything, it's that Undertaker is far from dead. Countless men have tried to bury The Deadman over the years; others hoped to replace him. But when it comes to WWE's greatest gunslinger, not even the ultimate blaze of glory can put him down.

CAREER TIMELINE

MARCH 24, 1991
WrestleMania VII:
Undertaker starts his
WrestleMania undefeated
streak by defeating Jimmy
"Superfly" Snuka.

AUGUST 26, 1991
SummerSlam: Undertaker
and Jake "The Snake"
Roberts crash the wedding
reception of Randy
"Macho Man" Savage
and Miss Elizabeth.

NOVEMBER 27, 1991
Survivor Series:
Undertaker defeats
Hulk Hogan for the
WWE Championship.

FEBRUARY 8, 1992
*Saturday Night's Main
Event:* Undertaker
stops Jake Roberts from
attacking Randy Savage
and Miss Elizabeth.

APRIL 5, 1992
WrestleMania VIII:
Undertaker defeats
Jake Roberts to go 2-0
at *WrestleMania.*

NOVEMBER 25, 1992
Survivor Series:
Undertaker defeats
Kamala in the first-ever
Coffin Match.

JANUARY 11, 1993
Raw: Undertaker defeats
Damien Demento in the
first-ever *Raw* main event.

APRIL 4, 1993
WrestleMania IX:
Undertaker defeats Giant
Gonzales to go 3-0 at
WrestleMania.

NOVEMBER 22, 1990
Survivor Series:
Undertaker debuts.

1990   1991   1992   1993

April 5, 1992, *WrestleMania VIII*

April 2, 1995, *WrestleMania XI*

JANUARY 22, 1994
Royal Rumble: Undertaker levitates to the ceiling after losing a Casket Match to Yokozuna.

AUGUST 29, 1994
SummerSlam: Undertaker defeats Ted DiBiase's faux Undertaker.

NOVEMBER 23, 1994
Survivor Series: Undertaker defeats Yokozuna in a Casket Match.

APRIL 2, 1995
WrestleMania XI: Undertaker defeats King Kong Bundy to go 4-0 at *WrestleMania*.

DECEMBER 17, 1995
In Your House: Season's Beatings: Undertaker repossesses the remnants of the urn after defeating King Mabel in a Casket Match.

MARCH 30, 1996
Slammy Awards: Undertaker wins the Slammy Award for WWE's Greatest Hit.

MARCH 31, 1996
WrestleMania XII: Undertaker defeats Diesel to go 5-0 at *WrestleMania*.

AUGUST 18, 1996
SummerSlam: Paul Bearer turns on Undertaker, helping Mankind defeat The Deadman in the first-ever Boiler Room Brawl.

OCTOBER 20, 1996
In Your House: Buried Alive: Undertaker defeats Mankind in the first-ever Buried Alive Match.

1994   1995   1996

July 26, 1998, *In Your House*

March 28, 1999, *WrestleMania XV*

MARCH 21, 1997
Slammy Awards:
Undertaker wins the
Slammy Award for Best
Tattoo, Best Entrance,
and Star of the
Highest Magnitude.

MARCH 23, 1997
WrestleMania 13:
Undertaker defeats
Sycho Sid for the WWE
Championship and to go
6-0 at *WrestleMania*.

OCTOBER 5, 1997
*In Your House: Badd
Blood:* Shawn Michaels
defeats Undertaker in the
first-ever Hell in a Cell
Match after a debuting
Kane interferes.

JANUARY 18, 1998
Royal Rumble: Kane locks
Undertaker in a casket and
sets it on fire.

MARCH 29, 1998
WrestleMania XIV:
Undertaker defeats Kane to
go 7-0 at *WrestleMania*.

APRIL 26, 1998
*In Your House:
Unforgiven:* Undertaker
defeats Kane in the
first-ever Inferno Match.

JUNE 28, 1998
King of the Ring:
Undertaker defeats
Mankind in a Hell in a Cell
Match after throwing him
both off and through the
top of the Cell.

JULY 26, 1998
*In Your House: Fully
Loaded:* Undertaker
and Stone Cold Steve
Austin defeat Kane and
Mankind for the World Tag
Team Championship.

OCTOBER 19, 1998
Raw: Undertaker admits
to setting the fire that
claimed the lives of
his parents.

DECEMBER 13, 1998
*In Your House: Rock
Bottom:* Stone Cold Steve
Austin defeats Undertaker
in a Buried Alive Match

FEBRUARY 22, 1999
Raw: Undertaker defeats
Kane in an Inferno Match.

MARCH 28, 1999
WrestleMania XV:
Undertaker defeats Big
Boss Man in a Hell in
a Cell Match to go 8-0
at *WrestleMania*.

APRIL 25, 1999
Backlash: Undertaker drives
off in a limousine, abducting
Stephanie McMahon.

APRIL 26, 1999
Raw: Undertaker attempts
to join Stephanie McMahon
in unholy matrimony.

APRIL 29, 1999
SmackDown: Undertaker's
Ministry of Darkness merges
with The Corporation to form
The Corporate Ministry.

MAY 23, 1999
Over the Edge:
Undertaker defeats Stone
Cold Steve Austin for the
WWE Championship.

AUGUST 22, 1999
SummerSlam: Undertaker
and Big Show defeat X-Pac
and Kane for the World Tag
Team Championship.

SEPTEMBER 9, 1999
SmackDown: Undertaker
and Big Show defeat
The Rock and Mankind
in a Buried Alive Match
for the World Tag
Team Championship.

SEPTEMBER 23, 1999
SmackDown: Undertaker
walks out of WWE after
refusing to participate in a
Casket Match against Triple H.

1997   1998   1999

MAY 21, 2000
Judgment Day:
Undertaker returns as the
American Bad Ass.

DECEMBER 10, 2000
Armageddon: Undertaker
throws Rikishi off the top of
Hell in a Cell

DECEMBER 18, 2000
Raw: Undertaker and The
Rock defeat Edge and
Christian for the World Tag
Team Championship.

APRIL 1, 2001
WrestleMania X-Seven:
Undertaker defeats Triple H
to go 9-0 at *WrestleMania*.

APRIL 19, 2001
SmackDown: Undertaker
and Kane defeat Edge and
Christian for the World Tag
Team Championship.

AUGUST 9, 2001
SmackDown: Undertaker
and Kane defeat Chuck
Palumbo and Sean
O'Haire for the WCW Tag
Team Championship.

AUGUST 19, 2001
SummerSlam: Undertaker
and Kane defeat Diamond
Dallas Page and Kanyon in
a Steel Cage Match to unify
the WWE World and WCW
Tag Team Championships.

NOVEMBER 26, 2001
Raw: Undertaker forces Jim
Ross to join Mr. McMahon's
Kiss My Ass Club.

DECEMBER 9, 2001
Vengeance:
Undertaker defeats
Rob Van Dam for the
Hardcore Championship.

MARCH 17, 2002
WrestleMania X8:
Undertaker defeats
Ric Flair to go 10-0
at *WrestleMania*.

MAY 19, 2002
Judgment Day:
Undertaker defeats
Hulk Hogan for the
WWE Championship.

OCTOBER 20, 2002
No Mercy: Brock Lesnar
defeats Undertaker in a
Hell in a Cell match.

2000   2001   2002

October 9, 2005, *No Mercy*

APRIL 3, 2005
WrestleMania 21:
Undertaker defeats
Randy Orton to go 13-0
at *WrestleMania*.

OCTOBER 9, 2005
No Mercy: After defeating
Undertaker in a Handicap
Casket Match, Randy
and Bob Orton lock The
Deadman in a casket and
set it on fire.

MARCH 30, 2003
WrestleMania XIX:
Undertaker defeats Big
Show and A-Train to go
11-0 at *WrestleMania*.

NOVEMBER 16, 2003
Survivor Series:
Mr. McMahon defeats
Undertaker in a Buried
Alive Match.

MARCH 14, 2004
WrestleMania XX:
Undertaker defeats Kane to
go 12-0 at *WrestleMania*.

JUNE 27, 2004
*The Great American
Bash:* After defeating
The Dudleys, Undertaker
buries Paul Bearer in a
concrete crypt.

DECEMBER 18, 2005
Armageddon: Undertaker
defeats Randy Orton in a
Hell in a Cell match.

2003

2004

2005

March 30, 2008, *WrestleMania XXIV*

APRIL 2, 2006
WrestleMania 22:
Undertaker defeats Mark
Henry in a Casket Match to
go 14-0 at *WrestleMania*.

JULY 23, 2006
*The Great American
Bash:* Undertaker defeats
Big Show in a Punjabi
Prison Match.

JANUARY 28, 2007
Royal Rumble: Undertaker
wins the *Royal Rumble*.

APRIL 1, 2007
WrestleMania 23:
Undertaker defeats Batista
for the World Heavyweight
Championship and to go
15-0 at *WrestleMania*.

NOVEMBER 18, 2007
Survivor Series: Batista
defeats Undertaker in a
Hell in a Cell match.

FEBRUARY 17, 2008
No Way Out: Undertaker
defeats Batista, Big
Daddy V, The Great Khali,
Montel Vontavious Porter,
and Finlay in a No. 1
Contender's Elimination
Chamber Match.

MARCH 30, 2008
WrestleMania XXIV:
Undertaker defeats Edge
for the World Heavyweight
Championship and to go
16-0 at *WrestleMania*.

JUNE 1, 2008
One Night Stand:
Undertaker is banished
from WWE after losing to
Edge in a TLC Match for
the World Heavyweight
Championship.

AUGUST 17, 2008
SummerSlam: Undertaker
defeats Edge in a Hell in a
Cell Match.

NOVEMBER 23, 2008
Survivor Series:
Undertaker defeats Big
Show in a Casket Match.

2006

2007

2008

April 1, 2012, *WrestleMania XXVIII*

APRIL 5, 2009
***WrestleMania 25*:**
Undertaker defeats Shawn
Michaels to go 17-0
at *WrestleMania*.

SEPTEMBER 18, 2009
***SmackDown*:** Undertaker
drives off in a limousine,
abducting Theodore Long.

OCTOBER 4, 2009
***Hell in a Cell*:** Undertaker
defeats CM Punk in a Hell
in a Cell Match to win
the World Heavyweight
Championship.

DECEMBER 14, 2009
***Raw*:** Undertaker
versus Shawn Michaels
(*WrestleMania 25*) wins the
Slammy Award for Match of
the Year.

MARCH 28, 2010
***WrestleMania XXVI*:**
Undertaker defeats Shawn
Michaels to go 18-0
at *WrestleMania*.

OCTOBER 3, 2010
***Hell in a Cell*:** Kane
defeats Undertaker in a
Hell in a Cell Match.

OCTOBER 24, 2010
***WWE Bragging Rights*:**
Kane defeats Undertaker in
a Buried Alive Match.

DECEMBER 13, 2010
***Raw*:** Undertaker
versus Shawn Michaels
(*WrestleMania XXVI*) wins
the Slammy Award for
Moment of the Year.

APRIL 3, 2011
***WrestleMania XXVII*:**
Undertaker defeats Triple H
to go 19-0 at *WrestleMania*.

DECEMBER 12, 2011
***Raw*:** Triple H delivering
the Tombstone to
Undertaker and The
Deadman subsequently
kicking out wins the
Slammy Award for OMG
Moment of the Year.

APRIL 1, 2012
WrestleMania XXVIII:
Undertaker defeats Triple H
in a Hell in a Cell Match to go
20-0 at *WrestleMania*.

DECEMBER 17, 2012
Raw: Undertaker versus
Triple H (*WrestleMania XXVIII*)
wins the Slammy Award for
Match of the Year.

APRIL 7, 2013
WrestleMania 29:
Undertaker defeats
CM Punk to go 21-0
at *WrestleMania*.

APRIL 6, 2014
WrestleMania 30:
Brock Lesnar defeats
Undertaker, snapping The
Deadman's *WrestleMania*
undefeated streak.

MARCH 29, 2015
WrestleMania 31:
Undertaker defeats
Bray Wyatt to go 21-1
at *WrestleMania*.

2012   2013   2014   2015

INDEX

Senior Development Editor
Jennifer Sims

Lead Book Designer
Dan Caparo

Book Designer
Jeff Weissenberger

Senior Production Designer
Areva

Indexer
Ken Johnson

VP & Publisher
Mike Degler

Editorial Manager
Tim Fitzpatrick

Design and Layout Manager
Tracy Wehmeyer

Licensing
Aaron Lockhart
Christian Sumner

Marketing
Katie Hemlock
Paul Giacomotto

Digital Publishing
Julie Asbury
Tim Cox
Shaida Boroumand

Operations Manager
Stacey Beheler

CONSUMER PRODUCTS
Global Publishing Manager
Steve Pantaleo

Vice President, Licensing North America
Jess Richardson

Senior Vice President, Global Licensing
Howard Brathwaite

Executive Vice President, Consumer Products
Casey Collins

PHOTO DEPARTMENT
Josh Tottenham, Frank Vitucci, Jamie Nelson,
Melissa Halladay, Mike Moran, and JD Sestito

ARCHIVES
Archivist
Ben Brown

CREATIVE SERVICES
Senior Vice President, Creative Services
Stan Stanski

Creative Director
John Jones

Project Manager
Sara Vazquez

Cover Design
Franco Malagisi

LEGAL
Vice President, Intellectual Property
Lauren Dienes-Middlen

© 2015 DK/Prima Games, a division of Penguin Random House LLC. Prima Games® is a registered trademark of Penguin Random House LLC. All rights reserved, including the right of reproduction in whole or in part in any form.

DK/Prima Games, a division of Penguin Random House LLC
6081 East 82nd Street, Suite #400
Indianapolis, IN 46250

ISBN: 978-1-4654-3942-0

Printing Code: The rightmost double-digit number is the year of the book's printing; the rightmost single-digit number is the number of the book's printing. For example, 15-1 shows that the first printing of the book occurred in 2015.

18 17 16 15   4 3 2 1

Printed in China.

ABOUT THE AUTHOR
A graduate of Fairfield University, Kevin Sullivan began his sports-entertainment career in 1998 when he accepted a position within WWE. Over the course of the next decade, he played an integral role in WWE.com's content creation process, most recently as the site's Content Director. He also served as managing editor of WWE's *Raw Magazine*.

Sullivan left WWE on a full-time basis in 2008, but continues to work closely with the company's publishing department. His first book, the *WWE Encyclopedia*, became an instant hit and peaked at No. 8 on the New York Times best sellers list. From there, Sullivan teamed with Simon & Schuster to put out *The WWE Championship: A Look Back at the Rich History of the WWE Championship*. The 320-page narrative tracks wrestling's most prestigious prize from its first days in 1963 all the way up to today.

Sullivan also wrote the New York Times best-selling *WWE 50* book and co-authored the second edition of the best-selling *WWE Encyclopedia*. Additionally, Sullivan has penned seven children's books for WWE, including biographies on Undertaker, John Cena, and Big Show.

Follow Sullivan on Twitter: @SullivanBooks